Ensuring a Strong U.S. Defense for the Future:
The National Defense Panel Review of the 2014 Quadrennial Defense Review

<u>Organization</u>

EXECUTIVE SUMMARY

In the first half of the 20th century alone, the world experienced two devastating world wars, the rise of the Soviet Union as a totalitarian menace, and the advent of the nuclear age. This grim history and the threats to America and her interests following World War II prompted America's leaders to employ our extraordinary economic, diplomatic and military power to establish and support the current rules-based international order that has greatly furthered global peace and prosperity and ushered in an era of post-war affluence for the American people. This order is not self-sustaining; it requires active, robust American engagement and sustained contributions by our allies. To be sure, other nations have benefited and will continue to benefit. But make no mistake, America provides this international leadership because it greatly enhances America's own security and prosperity. (8-9)[1] There is clearly a cost to this kind of leadership, but nowhere near what America paid in the first half of the 20th century when conflict was allowed to fester and grow until it rose to the level of general war. Indeed, our policy of active global engagement has been so beneficial and is so ingrained that those who would retreat from it have a heavy burden of proof to present an alternative that would better serve the security interests and well-being of the United States of America.

Since World War II, no matter which party has controlled the White House or Congress, America's global military capability and commitment has been the strategic foundation undergirding our global leadership. Given that reality, the defense budget cuts mandated by the Budget Control Act (BCA) of 2011, coupled with the additional cuts and constraints on defense management under the law's sequestration provision, constitute a serious strategic misstep on the part of the United States. Not only have they caused significant investment shortfalls in U.S. military readiness and both present and future capabilities, they have prompted our current and potential allies and adversaries to question our commitment and resolve. Unless reversed, these shortfalls will lead to a high risk force in the near future. That in turn will lead to an America that is not only less secure but also far less prosperous. In this sense, these cuts are ultimately self-defeating.

The effectiveness of America's other tools for global influence, such as diplomacy and economic engagement, are critically intertwined with and dependent upon the perceived strength, presence and commitment of U.S. armed forces. Yet the capabilities and capacities rightly called for in the 2014 Quadrennial Defense Review, hereafter referred to as the QDR, clearly exceed the budget resources made available to the Department. This gap is disturbing if not dangerous in light of the fact that global threats and challenges are rising, including a troubling pattern of territorial assertiveness and regional intimidation on China's part, the recent aggression of Russia in Ukraine, nuclear proliferation on the part of North Korea and Iran, a serious insurgency in Iraq that both reflects and fuels the broader sectarian conflicts in the region, the civil war in Syria, and civil strife in the larger Middle East and throughout Africa.

---

[1] These numbers reference pages in this report.

These are among the trends that mandate increased defense funding. Others include the rapidly expanding availability of lethal technologies to both state and non-state actors; demographic shifts including increasing urbanization; diffusion of power among many nations, particularly rising economic and military powers in Asia; and heated competition to secure access to scarce natural resources. These and other trends pose serious operational challenges to American military forces. (14-15) Conflicts are likely to unfold more rapidly. Battlefields will be more lethal. Operational sanctuary for U.S. forces (rear areas safe from enemy interdiction) will be scarce and often fleeting. Asymmetric conflict will be the norm. (18-20) In this rapidly changing environment, U.S. military superiority is not a given; maintaining the operational and technological edge of our armed forces requires sustained and targeted investment.

In this report, we examine in some detail the growing threats from different actors in different regions of the world, and note the challenges they present to calculating an appropriate mix of capabilities and force structure. (16-20) To lessen risk in an environment that is becoming more challenging over time, it is important to err on the side of having too much rather than too little. We agree with the 2014 QDR's emphasis on the centrality of East Asia as well as the continued importance of the Middle East to our security in the 21st century. At the same time, we note that current conditions require renewed attention to Europe. Indeed, the rapidly evolving nature of security threats to America and its allies – as witnessed in the recent turbulence in Ukraine and the extraordinary deterioration of Iraq during the writing of this report alone – causes us to recommend revising the force sizing construct of the 2014 QDR: "If deterrence fails at any given time, U.S. forces could defeat a regional adversary in a large-scale multi-phased campaign, and deny the objectives of – or impose unacceptable costs on – another aggressor in another region."

Since the end of the Cold War, the United States has generally measured the adequacy of its force posture against the standard of defeating adversaries in two geographically separate theaters nearly simultaneously while also continuing to meet steady-state demands for American military capabilities. The 1997 QDR offered an excellent rationale for this two-war force posture construct. (25) Unfortunately, however, the international security environment has deteriorated since then. In the current threat environment, America could plausibly be called upon to deter or fight in any number of regions in overlapping time frames: on the Korean peninsula, in the East or South China Sea, South Asia, in the Middle East, the Trans-Sahel, Sub-Saharan Africa, in Europe, and possibly elsewhere.

We find the logic of the two-war construct to be as powerful as ever, and note that the force sizing construct in the 2014 QDR strives to stay within the two-war tradition while using different language. But given the worsening threat environment, we believe a more expansive force sizing construct – one that is different from the two-war construct, but no less strong -- is appropriate: "The United States armed forces should be sized and shaped to deter and defeat large-scale aggression in one theater, preferably in concert with regional allies and partners, while simultaneously and decisively deterring or thwarting opportunistic aggression in multiple other theaters by denying adversaries' objectives or punishing them with unacceptable costs, all the while defending the U.S. homeland and maintaining missions such as active global counterterrorism operations." (26)

Regarding force size and mix, we note the Panel had neither the time nor the analytic capacity to determine the force structure necessary to meet the requirements of a force sizing construct or to carry out the national military strategy within an acceptable margin of risk. We believe, however, the force structure contemplated in the 2014 QDR – much less the projected force structure if the current budget baseline does not change – is inadequate given the future strategic and operational environment. This judgment is bolstered by comparing projected end strengths with the much larger force recommended in the Department's Bottom-Up Review (BUR) of twenty years ago. Although our conventional capabilities have significantly improved since that time, so have the capabilities of our potential adversaries, and the security environment facing the Department twenty years ago was far less challenging than today and what is projected for tomorrow. That a substantially larger force was deemed necessary then is powerful evidence that the smaller force envisioned by the Department is insufficient now. (26-27)

We note that the 2014 QDR is not the long-term planning document envisioned by Congress because it was dominated by the shifting constraints of various possible budget levels. Believing that national defense needs should drive national defense budgets, not the opposite, we think Congress should task the Department to do a thorough review to address in detail, without undue emphasis on budgetary constraints, how the Department would construct a force that meets the force sizing construct we have recommended. (30)

Both the Department and Congress should find value in a review of the Department's needs that is not driven by the severe fiscal limits that constrained the 2014 QDR. We believe such a review would conclude that the United States must prepare for what will almost certainly be a much more challenging future. We must have an energetic program of targeted reinvestment in research, development and procurement designed to protect and enhance the technological advantages that are central to U.S. military superiority. Priorities for investment should include intelligence, surveillance and reconnaissance (ISR) systems, space architecture, cyber capabilities, joint and coalition command and control, air superiority, long range and precision strike capability, undersea and surface naval warfare, electric and directed energy weapons, strategic lift, and logistical sustainment.

In addition, we believe the review would conclude that the Navy and Air Force should be larger. The Navy, which bears the largest burden of forward-presence missions, is on a budgetary path to 260 ships or less. We believe the fleet-size requirement to be somewhere between the 2012 Future Year Defense Program (FYDP) goal of 323 ships and the 346 ships enumerated in the BUR, depending on the desired "high-low mix," and an even larger fleet may be necessary if the risk of conflict in the Western Pacific increases. (49)

The Air Force now fields the smallest and oldest force of combat aircraft in its history yet needs a global surveillance and strike force able to rapidly deploy to theaters of operation to deter, defeat, or punish multiple aggressors simultaneously. As a result of the budget constraints imposed by the 2011 Budget Control Act, the Air Force's Bomber, Fighter and Surveillance forces are programmed to drawdown to approximately 50% of the current inventory by 2019. In the panel's opinion, the programmed reduction in the Air Force's decisive enabling capabilities will put this nation's national security strategy at much higher risk and therefore recommends increasing the number of manned and unmanned aircraft capable of conducting both ISR and long range strike in contested airspace. (49)

We are convinced the 2014 QDR's contemplated reduction in Army end strength goes too far. We believe the Army and the Marine Corps should not be reduced below their pre-9/11 end-strengths – 490,000 active-duty soldiers in the Army and 182,000 active Marines – bearing in mind that capability cannot always substitute for capacity. (49)

As to budgetary matters in general, we certainly understand the fiscal challenges facing the federal government, but must repeat that attempting to solve those problems through defense budget cuts is not only too risky, it also will not work. Sustaining these significant cuts to our defense budgets will not solve our fiscal woes, but will increasingly jeopardize our international defense posture and ultimately damage our security, prospects for economic growth, and other interests. America must get her fiscal house in order while simultaneously funding robust military spending. Aggressive health care cost containment should certainly be pursued both within the Department and more broadly across all government programs. Our national health care system is cost inefficient and stunningly wasteful, and it consumes more than a third of the federal budget. We offer a detailed argument to support our conclusion that America will have a high risk force in the near future unless the Department receives substantial additional funding. (30-31)

Regarding the defense budget, resources and reforms, we note the Department already identified $400 billion of cuts in planned spending in 2009 and 2010 plus an additional $78 billion in reductions spanning five years for the Fiscal Year (FY) 2012 budget plan. In early 2011, the last time the Department engaged in normal defense planning, Secretary Gates proposed a budget for FY 2012 that recommended modest nominal dollar increases in defense budgets through the remainder of the decade. Given his repeated efforts at cost containment, we see Secretary Gates' FY 2012 proposal as the minimal baseline for appropriate defense spending in the future. (23) Unfortunately, however, the BCA and the conditional sequester effectively reduced the Gates FY2012 budget baseline by one trillion dollars over ten years. This is unacceptable.

Congress and the President have taken some limited steps to ameliorate the impact of these budget cuts, including partial sequestration relief, yet only $43 billion has actually been restored.

This is obviously not sufficient. We recommend that the Department determine the funding necessary to remedy the short-term readiness crisis that already exists and that Congress appropriate these funds on an emergency basis. (23-25) The U.S. military's dangerous and growing budget-driven readiness challenges demand immediate action. The longer Joint Force readiness is allowed to deteriorate, the more money will be required to restore it. Congress and the President should repeal the Budget Control Act immediately and return as soon as possible to at least the funding baseline proposed in the Gates' FY 2012 defense budget. (25) That budget represents the last time the Department was permitted to engage in the standard process of analyzing threats, estimating needs and proposing a resource baseline that would permit it to carry out the national military strategy. Additionally, we strongly recommend that Congress restore the strategic decision making power that has been denied to both the President and the Secretary of Defense by the BCA. The across-the-board cuts imposed by sequestration have essentially prevented them from being able to align resources with national security priorities.

Innovation is mentioned repeatedly in the 2014 QDR. To be meaningful, the Department's innovation agenda should target deficits in capacity/capability, and be clearly defined, assigned, incentivized, resourced, monitored and tested. (49-50) Even then, it will be far from a panacea; significant additional funding is the needed cure.

Congress and the Department should not miss the opportunity presented by the current fiscal crisis to make real progress on the seemingly intractable issues of waste and inefficiency. This will only occur, however, with a stable appropriations process and consistent support from political authorities. Under current circumstances, the Department cannot be expected even to carry out its missions effectively, much less focus on internal reform. Make no mistake about it, however, the savings from a robust effort to tackle waste and inefficiency, though substantial, will not come close to addressing the Department's current, gross funding shortfall. At the same time, there are savings to be realized; it is time to stop talking about them and start achieving them.

The Panel believes that the costs of maintaining a quality All-Volunteer Force need to be reduced in order to avoid a reduction in force structure, readiness, and modernization, a decrease in benefits, or a compromised All-Volunteer Force (AVF). Thus, we applaud the creation of the Military Compensation and Retirement Modernization Commission and trust that its eventual recommendations will be fair to tax-payers, retirees, and current personnel without "breaking faith" with our national security or troops who need the best training, capabilities and support possible. Simply put, we hope the Commission will recommend and Congress will vote on sensible and cost-effective pay and benefits reforms that will continue to attract and retain the quality people we need throughout our force while reducing the pressure on readiness and modernization accounts. A key element of these reforms must be aggressive health care cost containment within the Department. The Defense health budget more than doubled from 2001 to 2014 (from $19 billion to $49.4 billion) and it continues to rise, with Congressional Budget

Office (CBO) estimates of $64 billion by 2015. At any given budget level, the increasing costs of health care are in competition with the costs of maintaining high levels of modernization and readiness of our forces.

Regarding acquisition reform, we agree with the recommendation of the 2010 QDR Independent Panel that Congress must fix the "current diffused, fragmented assignment of responsibilities without accountability with authority and accountability vested in identified, authoritative individuals in line management." The current fiscal crisis presents a good opportunity to get this done. The Defense Department must develop an acquisition reform plan that builds upon decades of solutions and establishes a clear roadmap to improve. To this end, we recommend a path forward based on clear lines of authority and responsibility, and more data-driven, evidence-based analysis to inform acquisition decisions. (33)

We also recognize the substantial savings that could result from another Base Realignment and Closure (BRAC) round and suggest a process for creating a consensus in favor of one as soon as possible. (34) Current estimates show the Pentagon has roughly 20 percent excess infrastructure capacity. Continued delay is wasteful.

Regarding reducing excess overhead and reshaping the civilian workforce, the Secretary of Defense should be given substantial additional management authorities similar to those available to Secretary Perry during the last major drawdown, including Reduction in Force (RIF) authority and meaningful levels of Voluntary Separation Incentive Payment (VSIP). Growth in the Pentagon civilian workforce is out of hand; since 2001 the size of the USG civilian workforce in the Department has grown by 15% to over 800,000. At the same time, the number of civilian contractors working inside the Department of Defense (DOD) has doubled to approximately 670,000. While some of these contractors are performing critical functions in support of the U.S. military, others are a legacy of the tremendous growth in the use of civilian contractors that attended the Iraq and Afghanistan wars. The Panel urges the Department to undertake a detailed examination of both the size of its civilian workforce and its reliance on civilian contractors in an effort to identify and eliminate excess overhead and right-size the civilian workforce. (34-35)

We offer some specific suggestions regarding U.S. force posture in the current security environment, highlighting the strategic value of forward-based and forward-operating rotational forces combined with responsive strike capabilities and prepositioned logistics hubs to sustain reinforcing forces based at home. (31-34) United States maritime and air forces with a broad range of capabilities should be operating across maritime Asia on a more regular basis, demonstrating credible U.S. combat capabilities, reinforcing international norms like freedom of navigation, and reassuring U.S. allies and partners of our capability and our resolve. The robust U.S. conventional force posture in the Middle East and particularly in the Persian Gulf region to deter Iran, reassure allies and maintain freedom of commerce should be maintained. This is even more necessary in view of the rising tide of violence in Iraq and Syria. And regarding Europe, the Russian invasion of Crimea and ongoing threat to Ukraine call into question the 2014 QDR's conclusion – a conclusion that echoes several previous reviews – that Europe is a net producer of security. If that is to remain the case, NATO must bolster the security of its own frontline states, especially in the Baltics and across southern Europe but also in Poland, lest they be subject to intimidation and subversion. America must lead the alliance in this regard.

America's strategic weapons today play an essential role in deterring potential adversaries and reassuring U.S. allies and partners. We therefore are quite concerned about the aging of the suite of nuclear forces procured in the latter half of the Cold War. Some units of our nuclear force are approaching obsolescence, and, indeed, some modernization is already underway. But it is clear that modernizing the present force would be a substantial cost on top of the already costly increase in general purpose forces recommended in this report. Our panel did not have the time or scope to study the nuclear force modernization issue, but we understand its importance. Therefore we believe that the impending nuclear force modernization program be subjected to a thorough review, including the assumptions and requirements of strategic nuclear deterrence in the present era. We recommend that Congress form a commission to study the recapitalization of America's nuclear arsenal in hopes that it might be freed from the malign combination of neglect and political whiplash it has endured since the end of the Cold War in favor of a sustainable program plan.

Finally, although risk is difficult to quantify because the world is unpredictable and capabilities are hard to measure on the margin, we conclude that American military forces will be at high risk to accomplish the Nation's defense strategy in the near future unless recommendations of the kind we make in this report are speedily adopted.

I. Introduction

The National Defense Panel was constituted pursuant to statute to assess the 2014 Quadrennial Defense Review and make certain recommendations to Congress and the Secretary of Defense. We have completed our task; our report follows. While our report is comprehensive and speaks for itself, we are compelled to emphasize one critically important conclusion in this brief introduction.

In our constitutional republic, the *use* of military power in any particular situation has been, and should be a matter of informed debate. But the *need* for such power has been much less controversial. Since the entry of the United States into World War II, there has been an overwhelming bipartisan consensus that all elements of national influence, and particularly the armed forces, must be robustly sustained.

The insightful report, "The QDR in Perspective," published in 2010 by the last QDR independent panel, contained an explicit warning: "The issues raised in the body of this Report are sufficiently serious that we believe an explicit warning is appropriate. The aging of the inventories and equipment used by the services, the decline in the size of the Navy, escalating personnel entitlements, overhead and procurement costs, and the growing stress on the force means that a train wreck is coming in the areas of personnel, acquisition and force structure."

This warning was not heeded. As our report shows, the defense budget cuts mandated by the Budget Control Act of 2011, coupled with the additional cuts and constraints on defense management under the law's sequestration provision which commenced in March 2013, have created significant investment shortfalls in military readiness and both present and future capabilities. Unless reversed, these shortfalls will lead to greater risk to our forces, posture, and security in the near future. In fact – and this bears emphasis – we believe that unless recommendations of the kind we make in this Report are adopted, the Armed Forces of the United States will in the near future be at high risk of not being able to accomplish the National Defense Strategy.

We are particularly troubled that recent budget cuts under sequestration were imposed without a comprehensive analysis of their impact on the armed forces and their ability to accomplish national security priorities. We understand that prioritizing expenditures is difficult in the turbulence of democratic politics where the urgent often crowds out the important; but we must emphasize that America's global military capability and commitment is the strategic linchpin undergirding our longstanding and successful strategy of international engagement and leadership.

Attempting to address America's budget woes through defense spending cuts is dangerous and ultimately self-defeating. In this economically interdependent but poorly integrated and unstable world, an America less capable of global leadership will soon become a poorer America less capable of meeting its other federal priorities.

We understand the approach taken by the Department of Defense in completing the 2014 Quadrennial Defense Review. The 2014 QDR presents realistic force structure choices that the Department will be forced to make at top line funding levels currently being projected. These choices were forced on the Department; at the prescribed funding levels, they will most certainly raise risk levels. In contrast, we did not consider ourselves bound by the current budget baseline; we assessed U.S national security interests and objectives, future threats, various force structures, and resource requirements and made recommendations that will enable the Department to successfully execute the full range of missions required by the Defense Strategy at a low to moderate level of risk.

Events are unpredictable; the more options presidents have available, the more likely it is that they can find ways to protect America's national interests using means that minimize the danger, or at least the scope, of armed conflict.

In short, Americans know that it is better, in a crisis, to have what we may not need than to need what we do not have.

In presenting this report, we wish to acknowledge our gratitude to the men and women who have served valiantly in America's armed forces. Their service and sacrifice have earned for them a greater measure of honor than our words could ever express. We had them in mind as we prepared this report, and we dedicate it to them.

II. Interests and Objectives

No nation can plan its defenses unless it knows what it is trying to defend and why. For that reason, we believe it important, as an initial matter, to summarize the history of American foreign policy in the modern era and distill from it, and from the actions of presidents of both parties, the strategic habits or principles that have animated America's engagement with the world.

The United States was never a completely isolationist power, but it is fair to say that prior to the two world wars, America played a relatively minor role in world affairs outside the Western Hemisphere. In the 20th century the world experienced two devastating world wars, the rise of the Soviet Union as a totalitarian menace, and the advent of the nuclear age. Some think this grim history might have been altered or ameliorated by greater American global leadership earlier in the 20th century.

That leadership came on the heels of World War II as America's leaders rightly understood that calamity as the outcome of a breakdown of global order, and rightly worried that another World War might soon result in incalculable destruction. What emerged was a new and enduring rules-based international order animated by American leadership and backed by its extraordinary economic, diplomatic, and military power. Recognizing the new global reality, our nation's leaders moved the United States to the forefront of world events, with a view toward advancing the core security and economic interests of the United States and its allies, minimizing the danger of a Third World War, and thwarting the spread of communism.

Consistently now for nearly seventy years, no matter which party controlled the White House or Congress, the United States has followed a policy of deep global engagement and leadership undergirded by a military capable of forward defense and effective global power projection. Americans judged that such a policy was the best way to preserve and protect this favorable international order that served their interests. We believe this logic still applies in an enduringly uncertain and increasingly hazardous world. This is because an international order favoring American interests and values – and those of our allies and partners and indeed all nations who wish to join – is not simply self-generating and self-sustaining. It cannot be left to the mercies of states and non-state groups that have different agendas. Rather, it requires leadership, global engagement, and military strength – and the only country with the power, credibility, and dynamism to play that role is the United States.

In particular, we believe there are five interests that should prompt America's continuing deep global engagement:

- *Defense of the American homeland.* The United States is best served by adhering to a strategy designed to reduce, deter, and, if necessary, defeat threats to the U.S. homeland before they grow in strength or metastasize. This is becoming increasingly important as the information revolution combined with dramatic improvements in global

10

communication and transportation have not only enhanced America's prosperity and quality of life, but have also given rise to greater global interdependence, facilitated transnational terrorist organizations, and made increasingly lethal biological, chemical, and cyber weapons available to both state and non-state actors.

- *Maintenance of assured access by Americans to the sea, air, space, and cyberspace.* America is and has always been a trading and travelling nation whose way of life, security and prosperity are significantly enhanced by peaceful access to the "common" areas of the world. Indeed, American prosperity is more and more intertwined with open and fair access to key regions such as East and Southeast Asia, Europe, and the Middle East. Yet in key regions of the world direct threats to the global commons are increasing as unilateral actions by stronger powers against their weaker neighbors undermine rules like freedom of navigation and peaceful resolution of disputes.

- *Preservation of reasonable stability in key regions of the world.* World War II demonstrated that America cannot isolate itself from conflict overseas that threatens our vital interests and allies. Both our security and prosperity are enhanced by peace and stability in key regions. This is a fundamental reason why America has remained actively engaged abroad since World War II. And since America is a military power without peer that has no interest in taking or subjugating other lands, its forward military presence and commitments to allies have greatly lessened the likelihood of arms races and damaging military competitions among regional rivals. Absent America's leadership, large parts of the world would likely evolve to dangerous imbalances, particularly in Eurasia, threatening American trade and investment, and potentially leading to conflicts greatly damaging to the United States.

- *Protection and promotion of an international order favorable to American interests and values.* Americans have benefited greatly from the international order that the United States helped create and sustain following World War II. As we note above, this order is not self-sustaining; it requires U.S. involvement, engagement, and active leadership, including a defense posture that underpins its continued vitality.

- *Support of global common goods such as combating disease, responding to disasters, and protecting the environment.* The increasing interconnectedness of the planet means that the United States has a national interest in global health initiatives, providing humanitarian aid, and responding to international disasters. Americans will be directly affected, for example, if the SARS virus breaks loose or if a humanitarian disaster in the Western Hemisphere leads to a mass migration. While most of the tools for dealing with these problems are non-military in nature, the military instrument nonetheless remains important to projecting effective capability to address these challenges.

In the years following World War II, the United States developed an architecture of global engagement designed to give its Presidents more options and capabilities in protecting these interests. In particular, the United States worked to build alliances, partnerships, and international regimes and agencies, created or expanded the various tools of "soft power" (trade and foreign aid) and sustained a much more powerful standing military than had been deemed necessary in the past. These tools of "hard power" have never been the only or the preferred means for deterring or addressing threats, but experience has shown that they are an indispensable element that increases the efficacy of the other tools.

In short, the United States maintains its armed forces as part of an integrated national security architecture, the purpose of which is to protect and advance American interests while deterring aggression and minimizing, to the extent possible, the risk of war. The effectiveness of America's other tools for global engagement is critically dependent upon the perceived strength and presence of America's hard power as well as our resolve to use that power when necessary.

Today, in light of resurgent regional powers in East Asia and Europe, the proliferation of nuclear and other weapons of mass destruction (WMD) in countries like North Korea, and the collapse of political systems across the Middle East, American military strength remains central to an effective foreign policy. This is particularly true with respect to our alliances and partnerships. The primary mechanism by which the United States has promoted its security interests and its leadership of the broader international order has been through the formation and maintenance of a wide network of formal alliances, such as NATO, treaties with countries like South Korea, Japan, Australia, Thailand, and the Philippines, and more informal but still deep partnerships, as with Israel and the Gulf states.

It is highly important for the United States to uphold these alliances and partnerships as well as to develop and expand key relationships by sustaining robust tools of power, including military capability.
Accordingly, the United States needs to maintain the military forces and associated capabilities required to provide credible security assurances to those allies and partners and to protect and sustain the liberal international order. We fully agree with those who believe that U.S. allies and partners should carry a greater burden, but they are most likely to do so if America shows it is willing and able to meet its commitments to them.

There have always been voices advocating American retrenchment. These grew following the end of the Cold War, and they are growing now in the aftermath of years of war in Iraq and Afghanistan. Many people advocate American retrenchment and question why U.S. engagement in the world needs to have such a strong military dimension. These people believe that the United States can avoid conflict and reduce its burdens if it disengages from its global responsibilities, the world it helped to make, and the international system it helped build and has guaranteed.

We differ strongly with such views. America learns from its past but looks to its future. Like all Americans, we admire and thank those who served valiantly in our military. They sacrificed to protect and strengthen America, an America whose global leadership and deep engagement is now more necessary than ever, not primarily to benefit other peoples – though others have and will continue to benefit – but because the United States is most secure, most prosperous, and most free if the broader international environment is stable and developing in a manner favorable to our national interests.

In this respect, we agree with the conclusion of the Independent Panel that reviewed the 2010 QDR:

"As the last 20 years have shown, America does not have the option of abandoning a leadership role in support of its national interests. Those interests are vital to the security of the United States. Failure to anticipate and manage the conflicts that threaten those interests—to thoughtfully exploit the options in support of a purposeful global strategy—will not make those conflicts go away or make America's interests any less important. It will simply lead to an increasingly unstable and unfriendly global climate and, eventually, to conflicts America cannot ignore, which we must prosecute with limited choices under unfavorable circumstances—and with stakes that are higher than anyone would like."

III. Strategic and Operational Environment

We believe the next two decades will pose a range of serious threats and opportunities to the United States and the broader international system. A series of structural trends are putting pressure on the architecture of the international system in ways that will profoundly challenge U.S. national security interests. The diffusion of power among many nations and the rising power of Asia; shifts in demographic patterns from increased urbanization to the aging of developed countries; the rapidly changing geopolitics of global energy markets and the rapid diffusion of advanced technology to state and non-state actors are prominent examples. The pressures on the international system are growing while the barriers to entry are lowering for state and non-state actors to employ increasingly sophisticated means of violence. We note the continued threat posed by al Qaeda and its affiliates, and other similar movements, and are concerned that these trends will make it easier for these and other violent extremist groups to operate. The United States and its allies and partners must also confront aggressive state actors that threaten security and stability in their regions. China, Russia, North Korea, and Iran each pose different but real challenges to regional stability that require DOD to plan for plausible contingencies.

The increasing velocity of these security trends and regional challenges will translate to an operational environment that is more challenging than defense planners are accustomed to and will likely pose greater and more complex dangers for the men and women we place in harm's way. We are concerned that the Joint Force envisioned in the QDR may not be robust enough to meet these challenges within an acceptable margin of risk, that under current trend lines the risk is growing, and that the force will need to grow, evolve, and become more capable if risk is to be reduced.

We take note of the trends and challenges noted by the 2014 QDR as well as other assessments to include the National Intelligence Council's report *Global Trends 2030: Alternative Worlds*, as well as recent testimony from leaders of the U.S. intelligence community.[2] We believe the following overarching trends deserve particular attention from U.S. policymakers and the broader national security community:

- Wider access to lethal and disruptive technologies: Continued proliferation of precision strike munitions as well as unmanned and increasingly autonomous systems will have major implications for U.S. military forces. The spread of advanced cyberspace and counter-space capabilities will also generate significant challenges, as will the continued threat of nuclear, chemical, and biological weapons proliferation. Diffusion of these

---

[2] See National Intelligence Council, *Global Trends 2030: Alternative Worlds* (December 2012); James Clapper, *Worldwide Threat Assessment of the Intelligence Community* (Statement before the Senate Select Committee on Intelligence, January 29, 2014); Lieutenant General Michael Flynn, *Annual Threat Assessment* (Statement before the Senate Armed Services Committee, February 11, 2014).

technologies will enable regional states to put U.S. interests, allies and forces at risk, and will enable small groups and individuals to perpetrate large-scale violence and disruption.

- Growing U.S. energy self-sufficiency: The dramatic increase in oil and natural gas production in the United States could potentially provide the United States with a strategic competitive advantage within the next decade. The United States will import less and potentially become a net exporter of energy resources by 2030. Regardless of how much or how little oil the United States imports in the future, America will retain a strong interest in the continued stability of the global oil market since the global economy itself remains dependent on oil prices. For this reason, regardless of growing U.S. energy self-sufficiency, it will still be necessary for U.S. military forces to help ensure that global energy flows across and between regions are secure and uninterrupted to prevent large-scale supply disruptions with global energy price effects and to assure our allies and partners who remain dependent on these sustained energy flows.

- Diffusion of power and shift in global power centers: As developing nations increase their power and influence, the relative power of the United States may well decline and the center of global diplomatic, economic, and military power may shift from North America and Europe to the Pacific and Asia. Protecting U.S. vital interests and defending its critical alliance networks in regions like Northeast Asia in the face of increased competition from regional powers will require new approaches and capabilities.

- Competition for secure access to natural resources: Various demographic and environmental challenges including global population increases and climate change will increase tensions between and among states and peoples over food and water resources, as well as other natural resources. These tensions will become most acute in Africa and the Middle East.

- Urbanization: The percentage of the global population living in cities will continue to grow over the next decade and beyond. In 1950, 30 percent of the world's population was urban; today it is roughly 50 percent; and according to the National Intelligence Council will rise to 60 percent by 2030. Much of this growth is projected to occur in littoral environments. Urban areas are not the only place where future conflict will take place, however, U.S. forces will need to plan for operations in and around cities as well as in the austere environments to which they have become accustomed over the past decade of conflict.

These and other overarching trends will cause the global security environment to evolve with increasing velocity, certainly at a faster rate than America's national security institutions are accustomed to. We believe that these overarching trends are playing out in particular ways in specific regions where U.S. national security interests are clear, and thus can guide defense planners as they prepare to size, shape, and posture tomorrow's Joint Force.

The United States confronts a number of specific regional challenges that require the U.S. military to plan, posture, and prepare to defend America's interests, allies, and partners.

China: We believe there will be elements of cooperation and competition with China as it rises and looks to secure its interests, and that the United States should seek to expand and deepen cooperation with China when it can. At the same time, China's renewed nationalism and increasingly assertive unilateral actions, especially in the cyber and maritime domains, constitute a growing threat to the international order. Government sanctioned computer hacking and blatant industrial espionage coupled with a pattern of piracy and counterfeiting of U.S. intellectual property are disturbing examples of disregard for the open network of rules-based trade and commerce. Moreover, China pursues semi-mercantilist trade practices, arbitrarily manipulates the value of its currency, and abuses the privileges of WTO membership.

In addition, China's increasingly assertive behavior over territorial disputes in the East and South China Seas and its disregard for the rules-based international order suggest that the United States must prepare to deal with an increasingly powerful and more assertive China with which it will have serious differences in the security domain. China's assertive behavior presents the most serious long-term threat to stability and to the security of U.S. allies and partners in the region.

Taken by itself, the scale and sophistication of China's military buildup over the past twenty years is similarly of great concern. By 2020, the Chinese will have a Navy of close to 350 ships, composed mostly of modern vessels outfitted with large numbers of advanced anti-ship missiles. In addition, the People's Liberation Army (PLA) will have a large inventory of conventional ballistic missiles and air- and sea-based missiles capable of striking U.S. targets as far away as Guam. China is increasing its nuclear arsenal, improving its integrated air defenses, and upgrading its ISR systems. China already has highly sophisticated offensive cyber capabilities and is developing the ability to destroy or severely disrupt America's space assets in every orbital regime.

The balance of power in the Western Pacific is changing in a way unfavorable to the United States, and we believe that China's rapid military modernization is creating a challenging context for U.S. military posture, planning, and modernization. Budgetary pressures must not be permitted to impede those enhancements to U.S. military capabilities that are necessary to provide security to our treaty allies and close partners, and to ensure freedom of navigation through the maritime commons. And fiscal concerns must not slow or diminish modernization of U.S. air and maritime power projection capabilities necessary to protect our interests and allies in Asia Pacific.

China's military activities and investments have several implications for DOD , including the need to:

1. Develop new capabilities and concepts of operation to counter China's anti-access and area-denial (A2AD) strategies. DOD must ensure it can project power over long distances; penetrate advanced air defense networks; and sustain combat operations in contested air and maritime environments. This will likely require investments in new capabilities, both offensive and defensive, as well as innovative concepts of operation to extend the strike power of today's Joint Force. In particular there are low cost ways of increasing the costs to the Chinese of escalating any conflict. Among these is comprehensively hardening the U.S. Pacific infrastructure, something our allies in the region should be encouraged to help pay for. We should also develop appropriate stand-off and penetrating weapon systems, to include electric, directed energy and cyber weapons that provide counter A2AD capabilities, and graduated effects to help manage the escalation of hostilities. The Department should consider developing long-range, land-based cruise and ballistic missiles which can be deployed in large numbers at crucial choke points, another initiative that can be developed in cooperation with regional allies. There are other asymmetric steps the Department could take to increase our offensive capabilities, such as stepping up the unmanned undersea vehicle (UUV) program to assist in intelligence gathering;

2. Enhance and accelerate defense relationships with key allies and partners in Asia. DOD must help its allies and partners enhance their air and maritime capabilities and missile defenses; develop reliable intelligence, surveillance, and reconnaissance networks particularly for maritime domain awareness; and invest in next-generation technologies to ensure they can contribute more to regional security and be interoperable with U.S. systems.

Korean Peninsula: One plausible contingency that would be among the most stressing for today's Joint Force would be a war on the Korean peninsula or an internal crisis ending in the collapse of the North Korean regime. Two years after inheriting leadership from his father, Kim Jong Un has continued to consolidate power in part by engaging in brinksmanship with the Republic of Korea (ROK) and the United States. According to the Defense Intelligence Agency, deficiencies in North Korean conventional military capabilities have compelled Pyongyang to focus on its nuclear arsenal and ballistic missile forces. Serious instability on the peninsula would require the United States to deploy substantial ground, air and maritime forces prepared for combined operations with ROK forces.

Operational implications of a contingency on the Korean peninsula include:

1. The need to plan for rapid movement of U.S. ground forces within Asia and from the United States to reinforce forward stationed U.S. and indigenous ROK forces;
2. Close communications with Chinese political and military leadership to ensure a shared picture of the operational environment and reduce the risk of miscalculation;
3. Advanced planning to quickly employ precision munitions against key targets in North Korea to achieve objectives, minimize civilian casualties and reduce prospects for nuclear escalation;
4. Planning to secure the nuclear, biological and chemical weapons and facilities in North Korea to prevent them from falling into the hands of terrorists or hostile states.

Middle East & North Africa: As recent events in Iraq have made clear, the ongoing turmoil in the Middle East is worsening and the threats to U.S. interests are growing. These events call for a reevaluation of U.S. military posture in this critical region. Of particular concern, the combination of the civil war in Syria, the ISIS "caliphate" and the Islamist insurgency in Iraq is creating a dangerous basing area for terrorists in Iraq and Syria. As the 2014 QDR observes, "Syria has become a magnet for global jihad." Director of National Intelligence James Clapper recently testified that al Qaeda affiliates in the region have established training camps for as many as 7,500 foreign fighters "to train people to go back to their countries" or launch attacks on the United States.

More broadly, we are concerned that the threat of Islamic terrorism is higher today than it was on September 10, 2001. The war against al Qaeda and likeminded extremists is not over and in fact the continued unrest in the Arab world appears to be magnifying this threat. Gen. Martin Dempsey, Chairman of the Joint Chiefs of Staff, describes al Qaeda and its affiliates as a network that represents a "generational challenge, which is to say, 20 or 30 years." The dynamics associated with the so-called Arab Spring may take a decade or more to fully manifest, and DOD should ensure its plans and posture do not revolve around assumptions of access and presence that may prove unsustainable. Lastly, Iran continues to pursue capabilities that could enable it to develop nuclear weapons while supporting a number of Shia proxy groups whose activities aim to destabilize Sunni regimes across the region, inflaming Sunni-Shia tensions and increasing the risk of broader conflict. The civil war in Iraq is likely to raise the level of this tension. Iran is also acquiring a number of asymmetric military capabilities designed to control access to the Persian Gulf and prevent outside intervention in the region.

Specific operational threats that should guide U.S. planning include:

1. Iran's nuclear program and the threat this could pose to regional security;
2. The threat of terrorist groups using the sanctuary of particular areas in the Middle East, such as the Syria-Iraq border region, as well as in North Africa to train foreign

fighters to plan and prosecute attacks against the United States and its allies and partners;

3. The danger of attacks on Israel that could lead to escalating conflict and a more general war in the region.

4. Iran's continued use of terrorism and political warfare throughout the region and the increasing capability of its missile forces;

5. The threat to safe passage through the Straits of Hormuz posed by Iran's acquisition of more advanced military technology;

6. The threat that Iraq could descend into a prolonged civil war or disintegrate into three sectarian parts.

Russia: Russia's recent military intervention in Crimea and its continued attempts to destabilize Ukraine signal Moscow is prepared to use force and coercion to pursue its interests, including in ways that violate well-established international norms. While Russia's recent aggression actually reflects both its strengths and weaknesses as a European power, it is nonetheless clear that Russia presents a more serious security threat than was the case a decade ago. This is evidenced by the recent downing of Malaysian Airlines Flight 17 over Ukraine and Russia's continued efforts to destabilize Eastern Ukraine. Accordingly, the United States can no longer simply assume that Europe will be a net security provider. Europe will require more attention and a higher sense of priority from U.S. defense planners.

Specific challenges that should guide U.S. planning include:

1. Russia's increasing use of rapidly mobile and well-equipped special operations forces with coordinated political warfare and cyberspace capabilities to create new "facts on the ground," particularly in areas of the former Soviet Union;

2. Lack of adequate defense capability in major NATO countries and continued lack of investment in defense modernization, including in forces that can be projected within the region or beyond;

3. An intelligence, surveillance, and reconnaissance infrastructure in Eastern Europe that is insufficient to provide strategic and operational warning;

4. Reduced U.S. forces permanently stationed or rotationally deployed in Europe and available for rapid response to crises as well as regular training and exercises with allies.

Nuclear Weapons & Proliferation: On top of these challenges, nuclear weapons continue to be a threatening feature of the international security environment and, indeed, note that their salience in some regions may actually be growing. Several nuclear-armed states, including Russia, China, and Pakistan, are modernizing their arsenals even as proliferation continues, with North Korea obtaining a nuclear weapons capability and Iran developing capabilities that would enable one.

Moreover, a number of potential U.S. adversaries, such as North Korea, are giving increased attention to how they could use their nuclear forces for coercive leverage against the United States and its allies in a crisis or conflict. Given the lack of attention dedicated to conducting operations against a nuclear-armed opponent since the Cold War, this presents a significant problem for U.S. forces, which must be able to achieve their objectives against such an adversary. In addition, the possible integration of nuclear weapons with potential adversaries' advances in sophisticated battle networks, strike capabilities, and alternative delivery mechanisms would pose special problems for U.S. power projection and homeland defense. We are also concerned that nuclear weapons (as well as chemical and biological munitions) could proliferate more widely because of the trends outlined above. Of particular concern is the danger that these weapons could be acquired and used by transnational terrorist groups against the United States by attacking the homeland or our forces, allies, and interests abroad.

Technological Edge Key to U.S. Strategy

These structural trends and regional threats to U.S. interests become more problematic when one considers the arc of U.S. military strategy and modernization over at least the past quarter-century. In essence, since the early years of the Cold War the United States has made a series of strategic choices to create and maintain a dominant military-technological edge against current and potential adversaries. Unwilling to sustain and maintain quantitative equivalency with the Soviet Union or to rely exclusively on nuclear weapons to deter conventional conflict, the United States decided to pursue an offset strategy and invested in a qualitative military edge that served as a significant strategic advantage during the Cold War, the Gulf War of 1991, and every military operation to the present day. This strategy was the product of a decades-long concerted effort to invest in force multiplying advantages like stealth, satellites, computers, and precision-guided munitions, ushering in an era when the United States stood alone as a dominant military-technical superpower. But what was once a dominant competitive advantage has been eroding for at least three reasons:

1. The diffusion of advanced military technology and the means to manufacture it have accelerated. Capabilities in which the United States once enjoyed a monopoly (e.g. precision munitions and unmanned systems) have now proliferated widely and will likely be available to virtually all U.S. adversaries in short order;
2. Nations such as China and Russia have made concerted efforts to outpace and counter the military-technological advancements of the United States;
3. U.S. Government-directed research and development spending has been eclipsed by the private sector. Unlike during the Cold War, the U.S. government is no longer the leader in research and development spending. Many of the innovations that will give the U.S. military its edge in the future are being developed by non-defense commercial companies that may not see DOD as an attractive customer.

In fact, we believe this erosion of America's military-technological advantage is accelerating faster than many defense planners assume. With precision-guided munitions proliferating rapidly, the risks to U.S. military forces are rising in each of the plausible contingencies the Department of Defense uses to assess current and programmed forces. Moreover, the emergence of unmanned and increasingly autonomous systems and other emerging technologies is likely to cause another significant perturbation in military affairs. At least 75 countries are investing in unmanned systems and they are beginning to be employed by actors as diverse as Hezbollah and China. The combination of precision-guided munitions and unmanned and increasingly autonomous systems poses a significant and growing challenge for U.S. defense planners, threatening both our security and global stability. As Secretary Hagel has said, "we are entering an era where American dominance on the seas, in the skies, and in space can no longer be taken for granted." Significant investments must be made to maintain U.S. military qualitative superiority into the foreseeable future. Failing to do so sufficiently will put the ability of the U.S. military to achieve national objectives greatly at risk.

Operational Challenges Becoming More Acute

The structural, regional, and technological trends described above will all interact in unique ways across the global security environment, posing serious operational challenges for U.S. military forces, which must now plan for battlefields that are more lethal, conflict that unfolds more rapidly, and greatly restricted operational depth making sanctuary far more difficult to create and maintain. Described below are some of the plausible operational implications of the security environment that concern us.

> First, actors such as China, Russia, North Korea, and Iran are all investing in precision munitions and associated battle networks (e.g. communications, navigation, surveillance) that will make it difficult for U.S. forces to gain entry to and maneuver within areas that once were relatively secure. This trend is particularly acute in East Asia, as China's A2AD systems, particularly its long-range and increasingly precise ballistic and cruise missiles, will be difficult to counter with current or planned forces and pose serious threats to U.S. and allied airbases as well as U.S. naval forces. These systems are likely to continue to proliferate around the world, increasing operational risks to U.S. and allied forces within the global commons – in particular the air, sea, and space – the unfettered use of which is central to the stability of the international system.

> Second, these trends will likely continue to allow non-state actors and even individuals to prosecute more aggressive terrorist and criminal operations with attendant increases in violence. The 2008 attacks in Mumbai, India by the Pakistani terrorist group Lashkar-e-Taiba represent the kind of coordinated, high-tech terrorism in urban environments that

may become more prevalent as secure communications and sophisticated intelligence, surveillance, and reconnaissance technology become more openly available. Transnational terrorist groups that desire to attack the United States and its interests such as al Qaeda, its affiliates and even competitors are likely to employ such means in the future. Due to the proliferation of technology, groups that might have once posed little threat to the United States may be able to prosecute relatively sophisticated attacks. We emphasize that the availability of asymmetric weapons – and in particular cyber and bio weapons – means that, as the 9-11 attacks showed – the American homeland is no longer protected by its geographic isolation.

Third, these trends will interact in ways that make it extremely difficult for U.S. defense planners to assume any kind of operational depth during future contingencies. The extending range of precision-guided munitions, the increasing difficulty of preserving operational secrecy given cyberspace vulnerabilities, and the growing access to advanced weaponry for non-state actors and individuals will require U.S. and allied forces to plan for constant threats in forward operating areas. It is difficult to contemplate a contingency on the Korean peninsula, as one example, where U.S. or allied forces would enjoy sanctuary from attack in the theater of operations.

Fourth, the proliferation of guided munitions will increase the lethality of future conflicts. As the cost of guided rockets, artillery, missiles and other munitions declines over time, U.S. and allied forces are also likely to face far more numerous enemy systems of this kind across the full range of plausible contingencies, adding further to the lethality of future conflict.

Fifth, these trends are very likely to increase the velocity of future conflict. The proliferation of unmanned and increasingly autonomous systems in the Asia-Pacific as well as the Middle East, for example, will have a detrimental impact on the ability to maintain stability during a crisis, or to manage escalation if conflict erupts. These systems, combined with the proliferation of offensive and defense cyberspace and counter-space capabilities, will greatly affect the relationship between offensive and defensive military capability in key regions, increasing the risk that a crisis erupts rapidly into conflict before policymakers and military commanders have adequate time to react.

These structural, regional, and technological trends and their impact both on U.S. defense strategy and the operational environment for U.S. military forces will test the ability of DOD to plan, posture, and prepare for plausible future contingencies or simultaneous combinations of challenges to U.S. interests in different regions or domains. These trends should inform how American defense leaders think about future conflict, how they plan and posture our forces for contingencies, and how they invest in and modernize our military forces for a rapidly evolving security environment.

That said, we cannot be confident in our ability to predict the cause, timing, location, and form of future conflict. If anything, recent history offers a lesson in humility. Given this fundamental and enduring uncertainty, the Department of Defense must place a premium on being agile enough to adapt, fostering innovation in operational planning and maintaining a clear margin of error in both sizing and structuring the force. More than ever before, it is unwise to assume that the Department can determine the exact numbers and capabilities it will need in the event of conflict; more than ever before, it is important to err on the side of having too much rather than too little.

We concur with the 2014 QDR that "regional and global trends in the security environment, coupled with increasing fiscal austerity, will make it imperative that the United States adapt more quickly than it has in the past and pursue more innovative approaches and partnerships in order to sustain its global leadership role." As the following sections in this report will make clear, we are concerned that the Joint Force will be neither large enough, nor agile enough, nor technologically superior enough to meet the operational challenges the future security environment will produce.

IV: U.S. Strategy

As with its broad strategic objectives, the American tradition in military strategy has been remarkably consistent since the end of World War II: the United States has sought to secure its global interests by deterring adversaries and reassuring allies through a combination of globally-deployed conventional forces, more robust power-projection forces based in the United States, and nuclear forces primarily postured to deter the Soviet Union during the Cold War. By maintaining stability in key regions, protecting the important transit points of the global commons, and maintaining security commitments through alliance networks, the U.S. military underpins the liberal international system that has ushered in the present era of unparalleled economic growth and prosperity.

The 2014 QDR is largely consistent with this tradition, while reflecting the administration's assessment that the international environment has changed since the Department's last review four years ago. If the 2010 QDR was fundamentally a wartime strategy balancing near-term efforts to prevail in Iraq and Afghanistan against longer-term imperatives to prevent and deter conflict, the 2014 QDR addresses what it describes as "21st century defense priorities" built upon three pillars; protecting the homeland, building global security, and projecting power abroad and winning decisively when at war. In short, while we in general agree with the strategy outlined in the QDR, we are uncertain it can be executed under current budget realities. In fact, the broad-based strategy set forth in the QDR increases the demands across strategy, capability, and capacity, thus widening the disconnect between America's strategic objectives and the realities of budget constraints and available forces.

Cardinal among our strategic priorities is the continued "rebalancing" of U.S. forces and strategic attention to the Asia-Pacific region. These rebalancing changes are most apparent in the 2014 QDR's treatment of "building global security." In keeping with the 2012 Defense Guidance, the review reemphasizes the primacy of the Asia-Pacific region among U.S. security interests. Asia-Pacific primacy notwithstanding, the 2014 QDR envisions a continued engagement in the Middle East, but one that emphasizes counterterrorism operations while avoiding long-running irregular conflicts. Obviously, the review did not take into account recent events in Iraq. The review's approach to Europe, described as a "producer of security" rather than a consumer, does not reflect recent Russian aggression.

In this light, we also believe that the force-sizing construct described in the 2014 QDR needs elaboration. A force-sizing construct is not a strategy per se, but it is an articulation of strategy in easily understandable terms; it is an important and tangible expression of U.S. defense capabilities. There are four reasons why it is important for the Defense Department to craft a prudent force-sizing construct. First, it is needed to ensure that future presidents have a thorough understanding of their military force options to protect U.S. interests in an uncertain security environment. Second, it is a powerful lever the Secretary of Defense can use to shape the size, structure, posture, and capabilities of the U.S. Armed Forces. Third, it conveys the Commander-in-Chief's expectations for what U.S. military must be able to do in defense of U.S. national interests, and helps articulate the rationale for the defense program to Congress and the American people. Lastly, the construct communicates to U.S. allies and potential adversaries what the United States is prepared to do to defend its interests.

Since the end of the Cold War, the United States has generally measured the adequacy of its force posture against the standard of defeating adversaries in two geographically separate theaters nearly simultaneously and at the same time meeting steady-state demands for U.S. capabilities.

The rationale for the two war force-sizing construct was perhaps best expressed in the 1997 QDR:

"Maintaining this core capability is central to credibly deterring opportunism—that is, to avoiding a situation in which an aggressor in one region might be tempted to take advantage when U.S. forces are heavily committed elsewhere—and to ensuring that the United States has sufficient military capabilities to deter or defeat aggression by an adversary that is larger, or under circumstances that are more difficult, than expected. This is particularly important in a highly dynamic and uncertain security environment. We can never know with certainty when or where the next major theater war will occur, who our next adversary will be, how an enemy will fight, who will join us in a coalition, or precisely what demands will be placed on U.S. forces. A force sized and equipped for deterring and defeating aggression in more than one theater ensures the United States will maintain the flexibility to cope with the unpredictable and unexpected. Such a capability is the sine qua non of a superpower and is essential to the credibility of our overall national security strategy. It also supports our continued engagement in shaping the international environment to reduce the chances that such threats will develop in the first place."

We believe this 1997 QDR logic is even more compelling today than when the two-war construct was first articulated. The 2014 QDR strives to remain within the two-war tradition, but uses language similar to the 2012 Strategic Guidance: "U.S. forces could defeat a regional adversary in a large-scale multi-phased campaign, and deny the objectives of – or impose unacceptable costs on – another aggressor in another region." We believe that a stronger and more explicit force-sizing and shaping construct would recognize a global war-fighting capability to be the *sine qua non* of a superpower and thus essential to the credibility of America's overall national security strategy. In the current threat environment, the United States could plausibly be called upon to deter or fight in several regions in overlapping time frames: on the Korean peninsula, in the East or South China Sea, in the Middle East, South Asia, and quite possibly in Europe. The United States also faces the prospect of having to face nuclear-armed adversaries. Additionally, the spread of al Qaeda and its spin offs to new areas in Africa and the Middle East means that the U.S. military must be able to sustain global counterterrorism operations and defend the American homeland even when engaged in regional conflict overseas.

Accordingly, we feel it is imperative that as a global power with worldwide interests, the United States armed forces should be sized and shaped to deter and defeat large-scale aggression in one theater, preferably in concert with regional allies and partners, while simultaneously and decisively deterring or thwarting opportunistic aggression in multiple other theaters by denying adversaries' objectives or punishing them with unacceptable costs, all the while defending the U.S. homeland and maintaining priority missions such as active global counterterrorism operations. As part of this construct we also stress that even when engaged in a full-scale campaign in one theater the U.S. military does not stop operating in other theaters, although the operational tempo of all forces may well increase. During the wars in Iraq and Afghanistan U.S. forces forward based in and deployed to the Asia-Pacific, although reduced in capacity by the Middle East conflicts, kept up an ambitious schedule of engagement, exercises, and security cooperation with allies and partners, while Special Forces soldiers continued partnering with local forces in counter-terrorism operations.

In saying this, we wish to emphasize that we are recommending a standard that is different from the two-war construct, but no less strong. Our concern is that the threats of armed conflict have proliferated in the last generation, and the kinds of conflict for which the United States must prepare are much more varied than they were twenty years ago. In short, the logic behind the two-war standard is as powerful as ever, but we believe that logic should be expressed in a construct that recognizes that the U.S. military must have the capability and capacity to deter or stop aggression in multiple theaters – not just one – even when engaged in a large-scale war.

Credibly underwriting such a force sizing construct would require a robust mix of forward stationed, forward-deployed, and prepositioned forces postured for rapid response in key regions, most importantly Asia-Pacific, the Middle East, and Europe. This rapid response architecture needs to be backed by a global network of relationships, access and overflight arrangements with key partners, ready global response forces including global strike, a credible nuclear deterrent, and a viable framework for more rapidly mobilizing Guard and reserve forces. While the United States continue to pursue conflict prevention and cooperation measures, given the increasing strategic weight of the Asia-Pacific region and the growth and modernization of China's military, one of DOD 's force planning scenarios should involve the most challenging, high-end threat the United States and its allies face in the Western Pacific for planning purposes. Since detailed force planning is beyond the scope and capabilities of this Panel, we recommend that Congress ask DOD to spell out the specific forces and capabilities it would need to meet the requirements of this new and more comprehensive force sizing and shaping construct.

We also observe that U.S. strategic forces continue to play an essential role in deterring potential adversaries and reassuring U.S. allies and partners around the world. While the United States has successfully striven for many decades to minimize the degree to which it needs to rely on its nuclear weapons in its defense strategy and to seek mutual reductions in the number of nuclear weapons with Russia, they nonetheless continue to play a unique and crucial role. America's strategic forces must remain the credible guarantor of this nation's and that of our allies' sovereignty. We therefore strongly reaffirm the QDR's emphasis on the importance of a safe, secure and effective nuclear force, regional and homeland missile defenses, and a strong counter-proliferation regime.

Such strategic forces should not and cannot, however, be regarded as an excuse for failing to maintain adequate conventional forces. The U.S. strategic force should at the same time be structured and operated in such a way as to promote both strategic and regional stability and aid in efforts to stem the proliferation of nuclear weapons.

V. Budget, Resources, and Reforms

We understand the significant fiscal problems facing the United States government. We further note that the core of that challenge is the large and growing gap between the amount collected to support entitlement programs, principally Social Security and major health programs, and the amount being spent on those programs. Meeting that challenge will require reducing the cost of those programs, or increasing the revenue collected to support them, or both.

Unless and until that challenge is met, the shortfall in those programs will continue to pressure the entire discretionary budget, including funding for the Defense Department. The cuts in defense funding are, therefore, not a solution to the government's fiscal crisis, but a symptom of it. Moreover, the government cannot solve its fiscal challenges without the kind of prosperity that can only occur in a global environment that is, if not peaceful, at least stable; and we have already explained why robust American military power is fundamentally necessary to support a stable, normative global system that promotes American economic growth.

We have been tasked to make recommendations regarding the budget baseline which we believe will be necessary to enable the Department to execute its missions at a low to moderate level of risk. Those recommendations appear below. To put them in context, we briefly recite the history of defense funding over the last five years.

Five years ago and after a decade of hard fighting, the Department was carrying out with some difficulty its essential missions. In 2009 and 2010, then Secretary of Defense Robert Gates engaged in a concerted effort to cut unnecessary or underperforming programs and to create efficiencies within the Department. This was targeted to achieve reductions or redirection of $400 billion dollars in planned spending. On top of this, Secretary Gates pursued an additional $78 billion reduction in the F 2012 budget plan spanning five years. This brought the total targeted defense cuts to $478 billion (prior to the BCA).

In the spring of 2010, the first QDR Independent Panel issued its report recommending substantial and sustained increases to that baseline, with a special emphasis on increasing the size of the Navy and recapitalizing the equipment inventories of the services. The previous panel thought the funding issue sufficiently serious to issue an explicit warning in the introduction to its report:

> "The aging of the inventories and equipment used by the services, the decline in the size of the Navy, escalating personnel entitlements, overhead and procurement costs, and the growing stress on the force means that a train wreck is coming in the areas of personnel, acquisition, and force structure."

In early 2011, Secretary Gates proposed a budget for FY 2012, which recommended modest nominal dollar increases in defense budgets across the remainder of the decade. Whether the amounts Secretary Gates proposed were sufficient or not, his budget would have permitted the Department to begin increasing the size of the Navy and funding other modernization programs necessary to sustaining the technological advantage that, as we discuss elsewhere, is a key component of future preparedness.

However, later that same year the Budget Control Act and the conditional sequester became law. The cumulative effect of those actions was to reduce the Gates FY2012 budget baseline by nearly one trillion dollars over 10 years.

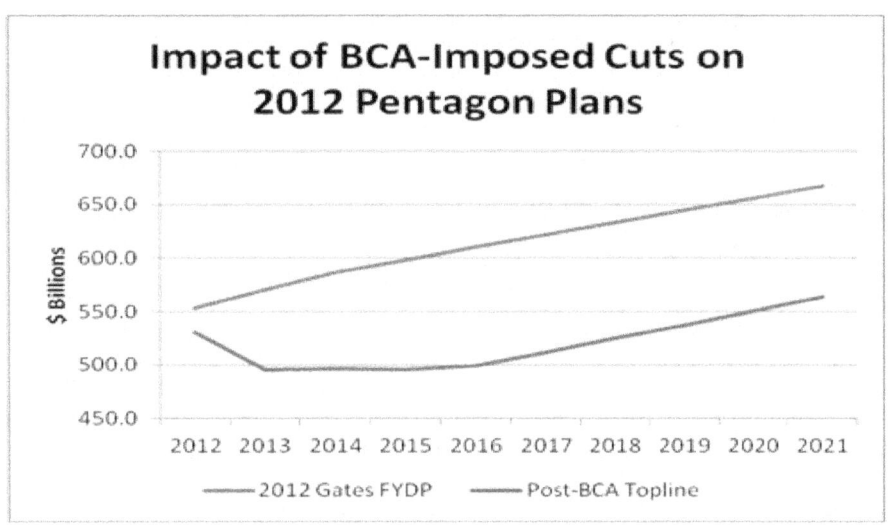

Secretary of Defense Leon Panetta assumed office in July 2011; the BCA became law in August 2011; and Secretary Panetta subsequently predicted that the reductions would be "devastating" for America's armed services. He did not overstate the case. Near-term readiness has dropped significantly, limiting the options available to the President. Moreover, at current funding levels the Department cannot sustain the procurement and modernization programs necessary to sustain future readiness.

Congress and the President have taken limited steps to ameliorate the impact of these budget cuts, including reaching a deal that provided partial relief of $44 billion since sequestration took effect in 2013. In addition, the President has proposed additional funding above sequestration in his current budget of about $115 billion over five years (in addition to $26 billion in the Opportunity, Growth, and Security Initiative in 2015). The House of Representatives has also passed a budget that would increase DOD funding by $195 billion over five years compared to sequestration levels. We applaud these steps, but much more must be done.

Including the 2015 budget request, the Defense Department has already lost $291 billion compared to the funding plan Secretary Gates recommended for fiscal year 2012, with $646 billion of still more reductions ahead unless current law is changed—bringing the projected total cuts to $937 billion. We want to make two points crystal clear. First, sequester has precipitated an immediate readiness crisis; returning to sequester levels of funding in 2016 will lead to a hollow force. Second, the increases above sequester levels proposed thus far, while desirable, are nowhere near enough to remedy the damage which the Department has suffered and enable it to carry out its missions at an acceptable level of risk. In fact, the capabilities and capacities called for by the 2014 QDR clearly exceed budget resources made available to the Department.

Under the circumstances, we recommend the following:

1. Congress and the President should repeal the Budget Control Act immediately and return as soon as possible to at least the funding baseline proposed in the Gates' FY 2012 defense budget. That budget represents the last time the Department was permitted to engage in the standard process of analyzing threats, estimating needs and proposing a resource baseline that would permit it to carry out the national military strategy. The reductions since then have been imposed with no analysis of their impact on short or long-term readiness. We believe it highly likely, given the events of the last three years, that the Gates' proposed fiscal 2012 baseline budget will not be adequate to prepare the Defense Department for the challenges ahead. But it is the minimum required to reverse course and set the military on a more stable footing. As an immediate solution, returning to the proposed 2012 baseline is the most reasonable response pending a thorough review of the Department's requirements.

2. The Department should determine the funding necessary to remedy the short-term readiness crisis that already exists. Congress should appropriate these funds on an emergency basis. The bill will not be small, but the longer readiness is allowed to deteriorate, the more money will be required to restore it.

3. The QDR contains many useful insights and recommendations, but because of the highly constrained and unstable budget environment under which the Department has been working, the QDR, taken as a whole, is not adequate as a comprehensive long-term planning document. Given the unstable global environment we have already described, a long-term plan is more necessary than ever. Congress should ask the Department for such a plan, which should be developed without undue emphasis on current budgetary constraints, and which should address in detail how the Department intends to meet the force sizing construct that the Panel has recommended.

4. The Department of Defense and the military services need budgetary predictability. The recent uncertainty of the budgetary process has been disruptive to programs, readiness, planning, innovation, and most importantly, it has had a negative effect on the members of our armed forces and the civilians who support them.

We emphasize that the failure to squarely confront the fiscal needs of the armed forces, and to provide a level of funding that is adequate to the needs of U.S. national security, is self-defeating in both the short and long term. In the short term, it leads to a readiness crisis that will cost more to remedy than it would have cost to prevent; in the longer term, it weakens a tool of U.S. power and influence that is essential to the peace and stability on which the security and prosperity of the American people depend.

Reforming the Way the Defense Department Does Business

The Department of Defense has been criticized for the way it does business. Many of these criticisms are fair, and the Department has recommended a number of reforms, only some of which it has been empowered by Congress to implement. The modifications are important both to save money and to improve the Department's long-term performance. Yet there are additional factors tying the hands of Pentagon officials and preventing them from achieving smarter outcomes.

First, insufficient funding levels for the Defense Department combined with years of fiscal instability have made it difficult for the Department to reform. The Department has been forced to adjust and readjust repeatedly to constantly shifting budgets determined without regard to requirements, and to operate without timely appropriations bills and on the limited authorities allowed by Continuing Resolutions. Under those circumstances, the Department cannot be expected even to carry out its missions effectively, much less focus on internal reform.

Second, the funding shortfall facing the Department is now so great that the largest feasible efficiencies will not come close to eliminating it, at least not in the near term. The QDR estimates that the reforms it proposed, if promptly executed, will save somewhere between six and ten billion dollars per year. This is a reasonable estimate. Certainly, achieving such savings and then capturing them for other uses by the Department is a worthwhile goal, but it is no substitute for increasing the topline in the way we recommend above.

Finally, we note that many of the most promising areas of reform will require additional statutory authorities, and all of them will require ongoing support from the White House and Congress. During past drawdowns, the Congress provided the Secretary of Defense with critical authorities to reshape and right-size the Department and its workforce, including authorities for Base Realignment and Closure (BRAC), Reductions in Force (RIF), and meaningful levels of Voluntary Separation Incentive Payments (VSIP). At a minimum, the Secretary of Defense must be given greater freedom of action and discretion in the management of DOD resources, both funding and people. The Secretary cannot be expected to reform the Department without cooperation and support from the political authorities to whom he answers.

Compensation Reform

America made a deliberate decision to employ a professional fighting force and to properly compensate service members for their time, commitment and sacrifices. The compensation and benefits offered by the Nation require periodic review and adjustment. In 2010, the QDR

Independent Panel recommended a Presidential-level commission to study holistic compensation reform. This commission is now at work. We believe it unwise to prejudge its conclusions. However, four years ago the first Independent Panel addressed the subject of compensation reform. We continue to support its basic conclusions:

- A failure to address the increasing costs of the All-Volunteer Force will likely result in a reduction in force structure, readiness, modernization, a decrease in benefits or a compromised All-Volunteer Force.
- To preserve and enhance the military, major changes will be necessary. This includes greater differentiation in compensation between one or two terms of service and a full career; shifting the emphasis of payment to cash over deferred or in-kind benefits; implementing a continuum-of-service model that allows service members to move fluidly between components and between the military, private sector, civil service and other employment; modifying career paths; and adjusting TRICARE to identify solutions that make it more affordable.
- To protect recruitment and retention, and to avoid upsetting the reasonable expectations of service members and their families, changes to benefits or compensation should be adopted prospectively by grandfathering in current service members and retirees.

We also recognize that balance needs to be achieved so that we can train and equip the force, as well as compensate and care for them. The nation must meet its two fundamental obligations to those who serve: ensuring they are ready, well trained and well equipped before being sent into harm's way on behalf of the nation, and ensuring their quality of life.

We note that the defense health care budget continues to grow. CBO estimates that it will reach $64 billion by next year. Included in this, the Defense Department pays a continually increasing percentage of beneficiaries' health costs as TRICARE enrollment fees, co-pays and pharmacy co-pays have remained unchanged while costs have increased.

We appreciate that Congress implemented increases to compensation and health benefits throughout the last decade in order to close a pre-existing pay gap, improve recruiting and retention and deliver promised health care coverage in order to maintain and care for the volunteer force during a decade of war. Now, with these fixes in place and growth stabilized, it is important to find ways to bend cost curves downward for both compensation and military health care.

Although it is beyond our competence to recommend a specific path to federal fiscal health, we encourage improving outcomes while reducing costs in health care. Federal health care expenditures, roughly one trillion dollars in fiscal 2013, consume more than a third of the federal budget. Studies comparing developed countries overwhelmingly conclude that the American health care system produces average health outcomes for twice the average cost per capita. For these reasons and others, many experts believe America's health care costs can be dramatically lessened while maintaining or improving health results. If they are right, health care cost containment would be among the most palatable solutions to our persistent and damaging federal deficits.

For these reasons and more, we welcome the Military Compensation and Retirement Modernization Commission report and urge Congress to give it careful and serious consideration, including passing any legislation necessary to implement its recommendations. We encourage the administration and Congress to rebalance compensation in a way that assures the most cost-effective path to meeting recruitment and retention requirements.

Acquisition and Defense Industry Reforms

Regarding acquisition reform, we agree with the recommendation of the 2010 QDR Independent Panel that Congress must fix the "current diffused, fragmented assignment of responsibilities without accountability with authority and accountability vested in identified, authoritative individuals in line management." The current fiscal crisis presents a good opportunity to get this done. The Defense Department must develop an acquisition reform plan that builds upon decades of solutions and establishes a clear roadmap to improve its policies and practices for both budgetary and modernization reasons. The nation cannot continue to spend huge amounts of money with insufficient returns or advantage to our Armed Forces. We note that the Department of Defense successfully instituted rapid acquisition programs during the last decade of conflict that contributed immeasurably to the success and survivability of our engaged forces. Given the unpredictable nature of future operating environments and the rapid development of technology, rapid acquisition techniques are necessary to respond to urgent needs of the Joint Force and to support innovative approaches to new challenges. We shouldn't lose what works. To this end, we recommend a path forward based on clear lines of authority and responsibility, and more data-driven, evidence-based analysis to inform acquisition decisions that will be made in support of both on-going operational and future out-year requirements.

Last year Congress began a reform initiative led by Rep. Thornberry to review and reform the acquisition policies and practices of DOD. We also recognize the recent Defense Business Board report on "Innovation – Attracting and Retaining the Best of the Private Sector" and advise that its proposed recommendations be followed. We commend the work of these groups and anticipate their insights will greatly inform the reform efforts of both Congress and the Department of Defense.

Another effort in need of support is the Defense Department's desire to reduce excess facilities and bases in the United States. Current estimates show the Pentagon currently pays to keep roughly 20 percent excess infrastructure capacity.[3] For some services like the Army and Air Force, the amount of excess is projected to be even higher. The Department believes it can save several billion dollars per year once a new BRAC is fully executed. We recognize the substantial savings that could result from another BRAC round and suggest a process for creating a consensus in favor of one as soon as possible.

These estimates deserve more respect than Congress has so far given them. No opportunity to increase the efficiency of the Department, and realize savings as a result, should be ignored. With the notable exception of the last round, previous rounds of BRAC significantly reduced the DOD facilities inventory and produced substantial and recurring savings for the Department.[4] That said, we have elsewhere recommended that the Department thoroughly review its requirements in light of our recommended force sizing construct, observations about force posture, and budgetary recommendations. That review may well lead to different conclusions about force sizing and posture than the Department has now reached. If after such a review, the Department still believes another BRAC is necessary, then we believe Congress should support it. With respect, Congress cannot insist that the Department justify every dollar it spends and then withhold support for reforms that will free up funds necessary for other higher priority parts of its budget.

In any event, cutting more bases overseas is not the solution. We note the Department is down to a bare-bones infrastructure already in key regions like Europe. The Army alone has already closed 100 installations in Europe since 2003 and plans on returning an additional 47 bases to host nations by 2015. Similarly, the Navy has been consolidating and shrinking its European bases over the last eight years. The Navy's European headquarters was relocated from London to Naples in 2005, while the service subsequently closed an air station in Iceland and support activities in Italy. The Air Force has reduced aircraft and forces stationed in Europe by 75 percent since 1990. Further overseas reductions in infrastructure could hamper crisis response times and ultimately extend the duration of conflict should it occur.

---

[3] The Request for Authorization of Another BRAC Round and Additional Reductions in Overseas Bases, Before the Readiness Subcommittee of the House Committee on Armed Services, 112th Cong. 38 (Mar. 8, 2012) (statement of Under Secretary of Defense (Installations and Environment) Dr. Dorothy Robyn)

[4] U.S. Government Accountability Office. *Military Base Realignments and Closures: Updated Costs and Savings Estimates from BRAC 2005*. Washington, DC: U.S. Government Accountability Office, 2012.

Additional changes are required to right size the civilian Defense Department and federal contracting workforces. Pentagon civilians have continued to grow even after the active duty forces have been shrinking for some time. From 2001 to 2012, the active duty military grew by 3.4 percent while at the same time the size of the USG civilian workforce in the Department has grown by 15% to over 800,000. CBO calculates that the rising costs of civilian pay accounts for two-thirds of projected growth in operations and maintenance spending in the next decade. Clearly, controlling or reducing civilian pay costs is essential to ensuring that the operations and maintenance accounts can be effectively leveraged to provide for the readiness of the Joint Force.

The defense contracting workforce is also in need of review. By 2012, the number of civilian contractors working inside the Department of Defense had grown to approximately 670,000. While some of these contractors are performing critical functions in support of the U.S. military, others are a legacy of the tremendous growth in the use of civilian contractors that attended the Iraq and Afghanistan wars. We urge the Department to undertake a detailed examination of both the size of it civilian workforce and its reliance on civilian contractors in an effort to identify and eliminate excess overhead and right-size the civilian workforce.

The Department of Defense may be the biggest unit of government in the world. Certainly, it performs one of the most important functions that any government performs. It is owing to the Department, and to the men and women at all levels who serve in it, to say that it has done its work over the years with faithfulness and dedication. But that does not mean it cannot perform better. With constant focus from high level leadership, with support from Congress, with persistence and patience, and with emphasis by all on accomplishing the Department's mission rather than protecting the status quo, much can and should be done to reduce costs while also better serving the American people.

VI. Readiness, Posture, Capabilities, and Force Structure

Declining Military Readiness Is the Pre-Cursor to a Hollow Force

The greatest advantage of the U.S. military is the quality of the people who serve. The professionalism, training, education and high quality of the men and women who comprise America's all-volunteer force are a core strength and national asset. We recognize that our current force has a high level of operational experience, strong leadership, and is generally well equipped based on the engagements of the last decade. An enduring comparative advantage of America's military is its high levels of skill, expertise, retention, and morale facilitated by its readiness.

Budget cuts result in unfunded capacity which, right or wrong, has led to reduced readiness. Today the Department is facing major readiness shortfalls that will, absent a decisive reversal of course, create the possibility of a hollow force that loses its best people, underfunds procurement, and shortchanges innovation. The fact that each service is experiencing degradations in so many areas at once is especially troubling at a time of growing security challenges.

The emerging readiness crisis has its roots not only in sequestration but also in more than a decade of war. After nearly 13 years of constant combat, readiness had dropped off in training for missions other than counterinsurgency. The ongoing requirements of presence, engagement and other demands on the force beyond Iraq and Afghanistan also accelerated the decline. It will take time and resources to retrain a force that is counter-insurgency centric, to now be able to address a broader range of thereat scenarios. In addition, two long wars led to tremendous wear and tear on some existing equipment, creating a maintenance and repair backlog in depots. Now, fewer funds than expected and uncertainty about forthcoming budgets have hurt the military's ability to recover from these readiness shortfalls. The Department needs more resources in order to generate and sustain the capacity demanded by the strategy – declining military readiness is the precursor to a hollow force.

This means the short-term readiness gap may become a permanent one absent time, attention, and money. In a recent statement to Congress, Marine Corps Commandant General James Amos outlined the mounting readiness challenges facing his Marines: more than 60 percent of non-deployed units are experiencing degraded readiness in their ability to execute core missions; roughly 65 percent of non-deployed units have equipment shortfalls and 35 percent are experiencing personnel shortfalls due to transfers of Marines and equipment to units about to deploy.

Similarly, Air Force Vice Chief of Staff General Larry Spencer's recent statement to Congress reported that the service's full-spectrum readiness began declining before partial sequestration, which has only worsened the problem. When automatic budget cuts took effect in April 2013 for three months, they caused many fighter and bomber units to stand down and pilots to stop flying. Today, less than half of the combat squadrons that were grounded have returned to their "pre-sequestration" levels of readiness, given the time required to re-qualify pilots and resume aircraft maintenance. According to General Spencer during his testimony to Congress, "This is not going to be a quick fix, and it will take us years to recover. If we are not able to train for scenarios across the full range of military operations, we may not get there in time and it may take the joint team longer to win."

If sequestration continues, the nation will have to fundamentally alter what it expects from its military. As former Deputy Secretary of Defense Ashton Carter warned last year, "if the budgetary caps, triggered at the same time sequester is triggered, are sustained, we're not going to be able to carry out the new defense strategy."

The first step to redressing the readiness gap is financial. The President has proposed additional funding of $26.4 billion in FY 2015, and $115 billion over the next five years, to partially restore military readiness. In FY 2015, the President is seeking money to accelerate immediate readiness improvements in training, maintenance and support. This includes increased depot repair work, more funding for fuel, spare parts and transportation costs, and additional training range support for the services.

But more needs to be done. Additional resources are essential to reversing the readiness slide. To repeat the recommendation made earlier in the report, the Pentagon should prepare a list of immediate readiness shortfalls along with the resources necessary to reverse them. Congress should in turn speedily pass an emergency supplemental to begin to restore readiness to adequate levels.

If a major crisis were to take place before the readiness is restored, the cost will be more casualties and more difficulty achieving key military objectives. The force must be reset, trained and prepared for the next conflict, whenever and wherever it may occur. If this is not done, it will impair the Department's ability to deter conflict and increase the length and human cost of any conflict that does occur. Congress and the White House should work together to address this unacceptable risk.

Force Posture

U.S. military forces must be sufficient to support forward engagement across the Asia-Pacific, Middle East and Europe, while retaining the ability to maintain deterrence and respond to crises and conflict in widely separated theaters. U.S. forces need to be appropriately postured to fulfill this strategy in light of an increasingly uncertain and threatening international security environment.

While the ultimate effectiveness of the U.S. deterrent posture depends on U.S. combat capabilities, forward presence through forward-based and forward-operating rotational forces is also an important part of U.S. strategy, especially in peacetime. During peacetime, in-theater forces provide concrete, visible evidence of U.S. commitment, reassuring allies and deterring potential adversaries, as the 2014 QDR notes. Such forward forces also promote and enable improved coordination and cooperation with allied forces, providing force multipliers for U.S. strategy. At the same time, it falls to forces based in the continental United States to buttress deterrence and achieve decisive outcomes in conflict. The military services must therefore maintain both ready forces for rapid response and also a mix of active and reserve components to achieve sufficient force, mass, and persistence when and where needed.

Concurrently, we recognize the need to further adapt the overseas posture of U.S. forces to meet new strategic realities, combining forward-based and rotational forces, ensuring responsive strike capabilities, and developing prepositioned logistics hubs to sustain reinforcing forces based at home. Given the uncertainty of the strategic environment, our commanders should be taking actions now to facilitate engagements with partner security forces and achieve greater operational and cultural understanding. Adjustments to U.S. force posture are needed across the three areas of greatest strategic concern and interest – the Asia-Pacific, the Middle East, and Europe.

- **Asia-Pacific.** The Western Pacific offers the most challenging likely theater of operations for U.S. defense planners. Accordingly, the Department is wisely shifting additional resources and capabilities towards the Asia-Pacific. The Panel supports this shift but urges greater focus on ensuring adequate and appropriate investment to ensure that the United States continues to maintain its military-technological advantages. At the same time, the Department should focus on ensuring increased combat-credible presence in peacetime and crisis to signal U.S. commitment, supplement deterrence, and reassure allies and partners.

  As we discussed earlier in the report, China's development of an increasingly formidable A2AD network of capabilities, as well as its increasing capabilities for regional power projection, indicate that the United States should ensure that it retains its military advantage and freedom of action in maritime Asia, especially in concert with U.S. allies and partners in the region. Given the growing technological capabilities of China's developing force, this will require substantial investments in new technology and operational concepts, as well as more innovative approaches to basing, access, and building partner capacity.

North Korea's development of longer-range missiles as well as nuclear weapons capabilities likewise puts a premium on strengthening the U.S. posture and alliances in Northeast Asia. Pyongyang's new capabilities, combined with its continued belligerence, have raised the prospects of escalation on the Peninsula even as they have made control of such escalation more difficult. We applaud efforts by the Department to work closely with allies like the Republic of Korea and Japan to strengthen our collective capabilities to deal with this difficult but intensifying challenge.

We also call special attention to the increasingly challenging and fraught environment in Southeast Asia, where U.S. allies and partners are embroiled in a number of tense territorial disputes with China. We note recent moves to station U.S. forces in Darwin, the plan to station a number of Littoral Combat Ships in Singapore, the improvements made to the U.S. facilities on Guam, and efforts to expand the number of exercises and access agreements with the Philippines and other regional partners. Yet the Panel is convinced that U.S. posture in this region needs to be bolstered further: naval and air forces, in particular, need to be more robust and should increase their presence in the region.

Thus, we believe that strong U.S. maritime and air forces, including but not limited to Navy aircraft carriers, surface combatants, attack submarines, maritime patrol aircraft, unmanned systems both above and under the water, Marine amphibious groups, and Air Force units with a broad range of capabilities, should be operating across maritime Asia on a more regular basis, demonstrating credible U.S. combat capabilities, reinforcing international norms like freedom of navigation, and reassuring U.S. allies and partners of our capability and our resolve. In this respect, the possibilities for expanded use of Australian and other regional facilities should be energetically explored.

- **Middle East/Persian Gulf.** The United States maintains a robust conventional force posture in the Middle East and particularly in the Persian Gulf region to deter Iran, reassure allies and partners, and maintain freedom of commerce. This robust presence should be maintained, although the precise force mix should be determined based on how the region evolves over time, in particular depending on developments in Iraq and whether Iran sustains or halts its support for terrorism or its pursuit of capabilities that will enable it to build nuclear weapons. If Iranian military capabilities improve and if regional partners seek greater reassurance, the United States should consider augmenting its forward posture in the Gulf region. Additional maritime, strike, ISR, and counter-mining capabilities would be especially suitable, particularly if the Iranian threat in the Gulf itself increases. If Iran's ballistic and cruise missile systems continue to evolve, the United States could look to further improve theater missile defense (as well as European and national) systems.

The United States should also ensure that it continues to enjoy base access, adequate supplies of prepositioned military equipment, and secure lines of communication in the region. At the same time the United States should continue its pattern of extensive and deepening security and counter-terrorism cooperation with regional partners, primarily Israel, Jordan, and the Gulf Cooperation Council states as the region faces growing challenges from religious violent extremism and political instability.

- **Europe.** The Russian invasion of Crimea and ongoing threat to Ukraine call into question the 2014 QDR's conclusion – a conclusion that echoes several previous reviews – that Europe is a net producer of security. If that is to remain the case, it is clear that NATO must bolster its own frontline states, especially in the Baltics and in southern Europe but also in Poland, lest they be subject to intimidation and subversion. We believe the United States must lead the alliance in this regard, developing a plan for a more robust presence in Eastern Europe and adjusting its force deployments accordingly. Specifically, DOD should consider enhancing its rotational presence and prepositioned stocks of equipment on NATO's easternmost borders while enhancing its ability to rapidly reinforce and support those forces. At the same time, NATO allies must shoulder a greater share of the Alliance defense burden. Lastly, the U.S. must lead a discussion inside NATO about the continued relevance of the limitations on NATO forces, both nuclear and conventional, that the Alliance took upon itself at the time of NATO's first round of enlargement in 1997.

These posture requirements will place a concomitant set of demands on U.S. power projection forces based in the continental United States and in "intermediate" locations, particularly in the Pacific. An enhanced posture in Southeast Asia, for example will place additional demands on and create new requirements for forces in Hawaii or on Guam, which would have to support and, in the event of conflict, reinforce forward-operating units.

In sum, the Panel recommends a fresh look at the posture requirements to fully support U.S. defense strategy in a dynamic security environment. A full assessment is beyond the capacity of the Panel, and the points made above are illustrative, not comprehensive, but the need to move the force in this direction should be imperative.

Vectors for Current and Future Modernization

The United States has long relied on technology to provide its armed forces with the capability and capacity to conduct a wide variety of global missions. However, the proliferation of technology, particularly information technology, threatens to put these traditional technological advantages for both the United States and its allies and strategic partners at risk. We therefore recommend an energetic program of targeted reinvestment focused on three key priorities: 1) bringing the best of the defense programs of record into service in a cost-efficient and timely way, 2) increasing investment in "transitional" systems – designs that harvest relatively mature and available technologies, and 3) developing emerging technologies that promise to bear more innovative and potentially game-changing results. Further, we believe that these investments must generally be made with an eye toward equipping allied and coalition forces; there should be a high threshold for developing U.S.-only systems, which should be procured only as rare exceptions to the general rule of building platforms that enhance partner capability as well as our own.

Moreover, research and procurement dollars should be protected from budget cuts and husbanded to preserve and enhance advantages in key domains of technological competition. Among them:

Armed intelligence, surveillance and reconnaissance (ISR) systems. U.S. forces have benefitted from decades of sustained investment into long-range ISR that provide detailed information to theater- and operational-level commanders and help U.S. forces strike first and with precision. U.S. leverage in armed ISR comes from keeping data standards common across domains and service boundaries. DOD is investing in both manned and unmanned ISR platforms and we believe both play an important role. An example is the Navy's manned-unmanned integration effort pairing manned P-8 Poseidon maritime surveillance aircraft with unmanned Broad Area Maritime Surveillance platforms. We believe that DOD must ensure that unmanned ISR platforms remain a generation ahead of any plausible adversaries. We thus recommend DOD continue to ensure that critical enablers of a shift into a more unmanned ISR regime are resourced appropriately—to include protected communications, autonomous control systems, and multi-aircraft control architectures.

Space. The United States military is critically dependent upon space for a wide variety of missions, including communications; position, navigation, and timing; warning and assessment; and intelligence, surveillance, and reconnaissance. Without the highly capable space architecture that supports the U.S. military, its capabilities would be seriously diminished. Accordingly, maintaining an effective defense and intelligence space architecture is vital for the country. Unfortunately, U.S. space assets are increasingly vulnerable or aging. We therefore recommend that the Department focus substantial effort and investment on developing a space architecture that is well suited for the much more challenging military environment that is emerging. This means a space architecture that is both highly capable and, given the growing threats to our space assets, resilient and durable in the face of attack. Space launch is a critical part of this architecture and there are emerging opportunities for commercial partnership as the private sector grows. This could be especially critical in view of the current challenge to using the Russian RD-180 engine.

The United States also needs effective ways to deter and counter attacks on its own space assets, and we therefore recommend that the Department pay special attention to this problem, including through both symmetrical and asymmetrical means. This includes where feasible working with technologically sophisticated allies and partners to share the costs of protecting mutually beneficial space assets. Of particular concern are space-based communications systems that provide the primary wartime information path to deployed forces. MILSATCOM systems have met the needs of the war-fighter well up to now; however, in today's increasingly joint warfighting environment a more decentralized, distributed and interoperable architecture may be in order for DOD satellite communications. DOD should also explore ways to enhance resilience by networking distributed space-based and air-based systems. Finally, in light of the development of potential adversary military space networks, we recommend that the Department begin developing operational concepts for how to hold such networks at risk.

Cyberspace. It is difficult to overstate the U.S. military's reliance on cyberspace, which is increasingly vital to the operations of U.S. forces. As this reliance grows, so too will both vulnerabilities and opportunities. As a consequence, the United States military absolutely must be able to act effectively in cyberspace – this will include both ensuring the adequacy of our cyber capabilities but also ensuring the resiliency and effectiveness of U.S. forces in a contested cyber environment. The Department is aware of this challenge and is already prioritizing investments in both offensive and defensive cyber capabilities, and in equipping the force for a contested cyber environment. We applaud these efforts, and urge the Department to continue to place such efforts at the forefront of U.S. defense technology investments. Indeed, we view cyber as among the very top priorities for the modernization of the force. Accordingly, we urge the Department to look beyond traditional avenues of modernization and leverage the contributions of the non-defense private sector.

Joint and coalition command and control. Two of the cardinal virtues of American military strength are that our Joint Force is a whole greater than the sum of its parts and that the United States is uniquely capable of leading and sustaining military coalitions in concert with a wide variety of allies, from the advanced militaries of NATO, Japan, South Korea and Australia to newly reconstructed forces such as the Afghan National Army. These capabilities are the product of decades of investment but improvements are needed, indeed imperative. Across the Joint Force, the secure sharing of fleeting intelligence and real-time targeting information must be enhanced; this is particularly important for the realization of operational concepts such as Air-Sea Battle. Even more work will be needed to retain and improve the U.S. ability to provide command and control of coalition forces, especially in a technologically contested environment, where networks of partnering forces may be vulnerable to various forms of electronic attack.

Air superiority. Uncontested exploitation of the skies has been the signature "American way of war" since World War II. This has meant not only dominating adversary air forces and conducting strategic strike missions but also operating in concert with other parts of the Joint Force. The "age of American airpower" reached an apogee during the 1990s, particularly in Operation Desert Storm and the Balkans wars. Now this advantage is being called into question, not only because others are deploying state-of-the-art aircraft, but also due to improved air defenses and the ability to use inexpensive but accurate ballistic and cruise missiles to hold airfields at risk. At the same time, air modernization efforts have been plagued by unstable budgets and cost and schedule overruns. It is essential that Congress and the Department work together to keep vital future air system programs on track and on budget. In the longer term, the Department of Defense needs to develop new capabilities and new operational concepts, including those mixing manned and unmanned aircraft in a challenging technological threat environment.

Long-range strike. Given expected advances in the quality and proliferation of advanced air defense systems, a critical DOD modernization priority must be developing new, survivable, long-range strike aircraft to maintain the ability to operate from long ranges, carry a broad array of operationally useful payloads, and operate in and around contested airspace. Whether the aircraft is designed to be manned, unmanned, or "optionally manned," the need to bring such an aircraft into service by the mid-2020s, when modern air defenses will put the B-2 bomber increasingly at risk, is compelling. We are concerned that continued budget cuts and the resulting programmatic instability would jeopardize this critical investment.

We believe it is also critical to ensure that U.S. maritime power projection capabilities are buttressed by acquiring longer-range strike capability – again, manned or unmanned (but preferably stealthy) – that can operate from U.S. aircraft carriers or other appropriate mobile maritime platforms to ensure precise, controllable, and lethal strike with greater survivability against increasingly long-range and precise anti-ship cruise and ballistic missiles.

Undersea warfare. Given the threats posed by anti-ship ballistic and cruise missiles, as well as the air and naval capabilities of plausible future adversaries, we believe it likely that, over time, dominance in undersea warfare will be the *sine qua non* for maintaining stability and security in key maritime theatres, and for defeating high-end military threats if necessary. The United States has built and maintained a major comparative advantage in undersea warfare over the course of decades. We are concerned that DOD is not adequately resourcing U.S. undersea capabilities and urge Congress and the Department to pay special attention to maintaining essential U.S. advantages in this arena. The Virginia-class nuclear-powered attack submarine (SSN) is among the Navy's most successful shipbuilding programs and requires a steady level of investment to maintain its cost effectiveness. As the deadliest and least vulnerable vessel we now have in production, if possible, the Virginia class submarine build rate should be increased. Even the decision to increase the build would likely have an immediate beneficial effect on the Western Pacific, especially considering emerging A2AD threats to U.S. access.

Looking forward, developing unmanned underwater vehicles that can complement current U.S. attack submarines and nuclear-guided missile submarines (SSGN) will be critical. The United States must become the primary first mover in the shift to unmanned undersea systems in order to regain much needed capacity and retain a measure of maritime technological dominance in the decades ahead.

Surface warfare. Like air superiority, sea control and power projection from the seas are central to U.S. interests in both war – to project power at transoceanic distances – and in peace to secure the free flow of international commerce. The surface fleet has both a "presence" mission and warfighting tasks that are of critical importance, but the proliferation of A2AD capabilities are making the latter substantially more difficult. Accordingly, the Navy as well as the Joint Force must rigorously explore how to make U.S. surface vessels more survivable through innovative approaches to defending them.

Today, the Navy must rely ever more heavily on the DDG-51 Arleigh Burke class destroyer, which has taken on a missile-defense mission in addition to its strike, anti-air, anti-ship, and antisubmarine roles while the Navy systematically modernizes the aging Aegis cruisers. Moreover, the Navy's legacy anti-ship and land-attack cruise missiles require technologically advanced replacements. We believe the Navy and the Office of Naval Research (ONR) should continue prioritizing development of shipboard directed energy weapons as these could be game-changers in the future. The Navy should continue to focus clearly and rigorously on modernizing the existing fleet and developing future surface combatant capabilities that are effective, survivable, modular where possible, and affordable in light of the broader shipbuilding plan. We agree with the 2014 QDR in its desire for "alternative proposals to procure a capable and lethal small surface combatant." The Department will likely be able to leverage existing designs to produce such a vessel quickly aiding in both total ship count and future fleet capabilities and capacity.

The necessity of Strategic Land Forces. We agree with the 2014 QDR that ground forces are "an indispensable element of this Nation's ability to preserve peace and stability." Growing populations and greater urbanization mean that many conflicts will occur in and around major population centers, while others will take place in remote, austere and inhospitable locations. Success in this complex terrain will require substantial land forces to achieve control while avoiding collateral damage. Strike alone cannot deter or contain the most significant threats in this environment. Land forces must be capable of conducting a wide spectrum of missions including supporting civil authorities, responding to humanitarian crises, providing theater enablers for the Joint Force, countering the proliferation of WMDs, and defeating adversaries in high intensity combat operations. Forward engaged forces build partners, assure allies, gain understanding, and provide both deterrence and evidence of U.S. commitment.

Strategic Lift and Logistical sustainment. With a global mission set, the United States military faces an inherent problem of projecting power at long distances. If the repositioning of more U.S. forces at home continues, this sustainment challenge will only increase. In an age of precision weapons and growing anti-access capabilities, long and large supply lines are increasingly at risk. Furthermore, as capacity is reduced, the American military has fewer lift and logistics assets. It is these enablers that provide both forward based forces and those in reserve in the United States with the agility to move rapidly within and between theaters to respond to crises or present clear and immediate deterrence to potential aggression.

As U.S. force posture shifts to reflect new strategic realities – whether measured in greater presence and capability in theaters such as Southeast Asia or even in Eastern Europe – so must the logistical infrastructure and mobility assets support new patterns of operation. We believe the Department must retain mobility and logistical capacity while improving efficiency in sustainment operations, and are concerned that, in times of budget austerity, such investments will be shortchanged. As forces are inevitably consolidated within the United States, there will be a greater long-term need for adequate lift and for sustaining the industrial base to provide such lift.

Electric & Directed Energy Weapons: U.S. forces are increasingly at risk from large salvos of guided rockets, artillery, missiles and mortars. This threat is particularly acute in the maritime domain, as U.S. surface combatants (particularly aircraft carriers) become more vulnerable to precise anti-ship ballistic missiles. Large U.S. airbases in Asia and the Middle East are also quite exposed to this form of attack. Conventional hit-to-kill missile defense technologies will struggle to respond to large salvos of incoming missiles, and the high cost per shot (at least $1 million for each missile interceptor) makes this form of defense untenable over the longer-term, as adversaries will be able to saturate U.S. defenses with far cheaper missiles and potentially unmanned systems. Electric weapons, such as electromagnetic rail guns and high energy lasers, have the potential to possess both high rates of fire and very low cost per shot, making them probable game-changers for U.S. defense strategy if successfully developed and fielded. DOD 's ONR has been at the forefront of developing these systems, early prototypes of which are already undergoing at-sea testing. Given the potential of these systems, DOD should not only protect their funding but also enhance it as soon as possible.

Force Structure

A precise calculation of the total force structure requirements needed to execute a strategy of forward engagement, leadership, global power projection, and homeland defense in the current and foreseeable international environment is beyond the resources of the Panel. The general characteristics of that force, however, can be understood. It must be capable of highly integrated joint operations and, as befits its global mission, must possess a wide range of capabilities on land, on the sea, in the air, in space and in the cyber realm. It must be durable, sustainable and powerful at great distances yet also globally agile. It must balance capability and capacity, precision and mass. America maintains this robust standing military power as part of an integrated national security architecture the purpose of which is to protect and advance U.S. interests, primarily through deterrence which is achieved through the combination of military capability and national will. Deterrence in key regions of the world is most aptly signaled by the presence of forward postured forces. The 2014 QDR is correct to emphasize the importance of forward presence in the Western Pacific, while at the same time maintaining adequate deterrent capability in Europe and the Middle East.

We emphasize that the United States does not respond to regional aggression just with forces present in the region. U.S. forces postured and available for crisis response include those ground, air, and sea forces permanently stationed overseas, certain elements of rotational forces periodically present in key regions, lighter, airborne forces flown to a crisis site where they are fleshed out by pre-positioned gear and equipment permanently stored forward, and heavier follow-on forces introduced in the event of more prolonged conflict. The United States also augments these force categories with air assets optimized for long-range global strike. It is important for potential U.S. adversaries contemplating aggression to understand that they face much more than just what they can see forward deployed at a given time. This is aptly illustrated in a place like the Korean peninsula where the United States maintains a force posture that would be augmented by much heavier joint forces in concert with the South Korean military in the event of North Korean aggression.

As active force levels are reduced, the chances increase for employment of those land forces in the National Guard and reserve as currently organized, trained, equipped, and prepared. The ability to mobilize quickly and effectively with the proper identification and resourcing of reserve component capabilities is a key hedge against uncertainty. To have reserve component formations properly trained, equipped, and prepared for rapid introduction into contingencies or most heavy combat will require higher states of readiness and leader preparation, as well as changes to our mobilization processes.

We believe that the QDR force is not adequate to meet these posture requirements, that the readiness of the force is rapidly declining, and that it will continue to worsen under the current defense budget baseline of sequestration. The U.S. military has undergone repeated reductions in capacity over the past generation. Notwithstanding the fact that modern systems, platforms and force structure elements embody higher levels of lethality and combat effectiveness when compared to their counterparts of 20 years ago, there remains a need for certain levels of raw capacity to meet the demands of the current and future security environment. Although much of our capability is based on a level of technological superiority, the capability gap between us and our potential competitors is shrinking.

We offer some cautions later in this section as to why superior capability is not always a substitute for capacity but perhaps the most persuasive rationale came during the course of several interviews with Geographic Combatant Commanders who clearly called for more capacity to meet the requirements of contingency plans, regional presence, and theater security cooperation and engagement. While we are aware that post-war reductions in overall defense resources are a normal historical pattern, for the reasons cited above, we believe the combination of BCA and sequestration cuts is having a perilous effect on readiness. The perception (correct or not) that the U.S. military is now a "smaller, less ready, less global" force could embolden challengers and encourage adventurism. This idea is addressed more fully in section VII (Strategic Risk).

The National Defense Panel reviewed multiple force structures, including the BUR force, the 2002 Force, the QDR force, and the sequestration force. Table 1 (Appendix A) contains a comparison of these force structures.

To further explain our assessment that the QDR force is inadequate, Table 1 illustrates the basic metrics of force structure since 2002; a sequestration-level force is inadequate in the face of the increasingly complex and threatening security environment we describe in earlier sections of this report. The table shows the forces under sequestration to be far fewer than what Secretary Gates felt were the minimum essential to address those same security challenges.

Under the BCA, automatic reductions of the caps on Government-wide discretionary funding (sequestration) will return in FY 2016 and continue through the remainder of the FYDP. Table 2 (Appendix B) highlights the impacts of these reductions on DOD by service and specific platform/system.

To repeat: The Panel lacks the time and the analytical capacity to fully describe the force structure needed to execute U.S. defense strategy, including forward engagement, timely and effective power projection to threatened regions, and defending the American homeland, at a reasonable level of risk. The Independent Panel that reviewed the 2010 QDR came to a similar conclusion, and in the absence of a solid force sizing construct, the former panel adopted as a baseline the force structure derived from the 1993 BUR, a structure that at the time had been thoroughly documented by all the analytics available to the Department. The 2010 NDP did so for two reasons: respect for the prior planning effort and the analytical work that went into that review, and the panel's conclusion that, given the increased stress on the 2010 force together with the additional missions assumed by the Defense Department since the mid-1990s, it was unlikely the United States could make do with less military than was needed in 1993.

We find this reasoning both persuasive and instructive today. The BUR was conducted at the beginning of the post-Cold War era, a unique uni-polar moment in which democratic capitalism seemed to be universally accepted, Russia was focused inward and not unfriendly, China had not begun its aggressive military behavior, North Korea had no nuclear weapons, Iran's nuclear ambitions were still not recognized, the 9-11 attacks had not occurred, and both East Asia and the Middle East were more stable than today. In other words, if a force sized at the BUR levels was necessary twenty years ago, when the world was much more stable and less risky, that is powerful evidence that the substantially smaller force of today (much less the even smaller force of the future under the QDR or sequestration) is too small. We are not suggesting that the BUR end strengths should be a straitjacket on defense planning – the Department may well conclude that a different mix of forces is preferable after conducting the kind of thorough review we recommend elsewhere in this Report – but we believe that, given proliferating security threats, any reasonable review will conclude that the Navy and Air Force should be larger than they are today, and that the QDR's contemplated reduction in active Army end strength goes too far.

The severe budget cuts of the last several years have presented the Department with a choice between needed "capacity" and needed "capability" – that is, between reducing a force that is already too small and cutting the modernization programs that will make the force more effective and less vulnerable. To some extent, a quality vs. quantity choice is always before the Department; even when budgets are adequate, the Department must decide whether to invest its marginal dollars in current as against future capabilities. In such situations, our own bias is towards investing in future capabilities, consistent with the Department's tradition, which we have already discussed, of relying less on numbers and more on the quality and readiness of its personnel and the technological superiority of its inventory and operational concepts. Protecting investment in the future is particularly important now when all indicators point to an international security environment that will be even more challenging tomorrow than it is today.

With that said, as the Department plans for the future, we caution against the belief that capability can always be substituted for capacity, for three reasons. First, while the United States is, properly, modernizing its forces, potential future adversaries are modernizing theirs as well. If the U.S. military's relative technological superiority is reduced, numbers will matter all the more. Second, even a highly superior force cannot sustain a sufficient global presence and deter conflicts in different theaters at the same time if the size of the overall force structure is not adequate. Finally, overemphasizing capability can put too much pressure on modernization programs to accomplish the impossible. The fewer platforms a service has, the greater the pressure it feels to increase the requirements for its remaining inventory. That tends to raise the costs of modernization programs, which eats up the savings that the service hoped to achieve by reducing its inventory in the first place. We note also that in the current budgetary environment, the choice before the Department is really no choice at all; the existing baseline will fully support neither the capability nor the capacity that the Department needs.

Therefore, we recommend a two-fold plan to rebuild a force structure with both sufficient capacity and capability to meet the demands of sustained American global leadership. The first phase addresses the urgent need for capacity by protecting and increasing force size while efficiently modernizing current formations. In particular, we conclude that:

- The Army and Marine Corps should not be reduced below their pre-9/11 end-strengths – 490,000 active-duty soldiers in the Army and 182,000 active Marines. Given the instability in the Middle East and the Korean peninsula, and the recent events in Eastern Europe, the Panel believes that it is imprudent to believe that the Army and Marines can be smaller than they were in the 1990s without accepting high levels of risk.

- The Navy, which bears the largest burden of forward-presence missions, must be larger: the fleet is on a budgetary path to 260 ships or less, according to Adm. Jonathan Greenert, the chief of naval operations.[5] We believe the fleet-size requirement to be somewhere between the 2012 FYDP goal of 323 ships and the 346 ships enumerated in the Bottom-up Review, depending on the desired "high-low mix." We caution that the number of ships may need to grow in the future should maritime challenges in Asia Pacific and the Middle East continue to increase.

- The Air Force now fields the smallest and oldest force of combat aircraft in its history yet needs a global surveillance and strike force able to rapidly deploy to theaters of operation to deter, defeat, or punish multiple aggressors simultaneously. As a result of the budget constraints imposed by the 2011 Budget Control Act, the Air Force's Bomber, Fighter and Surveillance forces are programmed to drawdown to approximately 50% of the current inventory by 2019. In the panel's opinion, the programmed reduction in the Air Force's decisive enabling capabilities will put this nation's national security strategy at much higher risk and therefore recommends increasing the number of manned and unmanned aircraft capable of conducting both ISR and long range strike in contested airspace.

- Once capacity has been adjusted, the U.S. military also needs to commit itself to a plan for technological innovation and operational experimentation. The desire to innovate – variously described in previous reviews as "exploiting the Revolution in Military Affairs" or "defense transformation" – has itself become a Defense Department tradition, and the 2014 QDR is no exception. "Innovation," wrote Defense Secretary Chuck Hagel in his introduction to the review, "will be center stage." We agree with this emphasis, but suggest that the Department has been – not only in the post-9/11 era but also in the 1990s – too often forced to divert resources and attention from future innovation to current crises. The only way to achieve a proper balance between near-term needs and long-term innovation is to sustain sufficient research, development and procurement investments and to incentivize concept development and experimentation across the services.

---

[5] Impact of Sequestration on the National Defense, Before the Senate Committee on Armed Services, 113th Cong. (Nov. 7, 2013).

Innovation is mentioned repeatedly in the 2014 QDR. The notion is appealing in a period of transition and declining resources. In a period of transition it is good to look for new opportunities – new ways to accomplish tasks, promising technologies that can revolutionize warfare, and operational concepts that can be more effective. At the same time, the QDR's innovation recommendations would employ unspecified, untargeted, and under-resourced measures in the hopes of gaining the necessary agility to mitigate strategy to resource mismatches.

In a period of declining resources, innovation can mean renewed emphasis on research and development or become a euphemism for doing more with less. Innovation is multifaceted: encompassing doctrine, technologies, equipment, joint approaches, organizations, and plans. If innovation is to be meaningful in the Department of Defense it must be clearly defined, assigned, incentivized, resourced, monitored and tested. In our estimation, joint war-gaming and analysis of operational concepts have declined. It will be increasingly important to build and support a culture of innovation at the service level, including creating opportunities to compete concepts, conduct real experiments, pilot and prototype new solutions, risk failure and learn as an organization. This will be no small challenge. In some ways the Department remains in denial about the reality of a new future and is still dedicated to doing things the way they have always been done. As an example, even after over a decade of joint operations in Iraq and Afghanistan there remains a need for better coordination and less duplication of capabilities across the services.

Nuclear Posture

The appropriate structure of U.S. strategic forces raises a particular set of considerations for U.S. defense planning. As noted previously, the U.S. nuclear deterrent plays a cornerstone role in broader U.S. defense strategy. Today, however, the United States faces the looming obsolescence of the suite of nuclear forces procured in the latter half of the Cold War. Nuclear force modernization is essential. Strategic force modernization should continue with the on-going programs for Long Range Strike and the replacement of the *Ohio* class of ballistic missile submarines. The Department should also review the viability of both the land-based and sea-based classes of ICBMs with an eye towards eventual replacement. After undertaking extensive analysis of future U.S. strategic force requirements in recent years, the Department of Defense recommended that the United States should maintain a triad of ballistic missile submarines, ICBMs, and heavy bombers at lower warhead and delivery levels. Accordingly, the Department is committed to a recapitalization of the triad, which under current budget constraints is unaffordable, especially considering that the nuclear deterrent's supporting infrastructure, command and control system, and other enabling capabilities also require expensive renovations.

This recapitalization will involve substantial outlays over the coming decades, and the merits of some aspects of this expensive recapitalization can be debated. Recapitalization of all three legs of the nuclear Triad with associated weapons could cost between $600 billion and $1 trillion over a thirty year period, the costs of which would likely come at the expense of needed improvements in conventional forces. The U.S. nuclear arsenal could be reduced in support of the country's arms control and nonproliferation objectives, although that would likely require complex and difficult bilateral or even multinational negotiations. Alternatively, the current structure of U.S. nuclear forces can be retained. Either way, America's nuclear arsenal will need life extension programs and some modernization if its deterrent value is to be preserved. Reasonable decisions about the appropriate structure for U.S. nuclear forces are crucial for developing and maintaining the lasting and broad-based political support the U.S. nuclear deterrent needs. Such support is critical to ensuring that the U.S. nuclear arsenal is freed from the malign combination of neglect and political whiplash it has endured since the end of the Cold War in favor of a predictable and consistent funding and authorizing horizon.

Given the existential importance of the nuclear deterrent, we recommend that the Administration and Congress urgently and jointly undertake a new study to examine the intellectual underpinnings of our strategic deterrence policy. We feel this is particularly urgent in the face of limited resources and in light of the changing international environment characterized by a multi-polar world of states possessing nuclear arms and biological weapons, either of which could pose an existential threat to the United States. This study should take into account the work done by two previous commissions, the Commission on the Prevention of WMD Proliferation and Terrorism (2008) and the Congressional Commission on the Strategic Posture of the United States (2009). Any consideration of reductions below new START levels should undergo a rigorous examination of its implications by the Administration.

Finally, we strongly believe that any future nuclear deterrent posture should continue to provide credible, effective deterrence and reassurance, including in the context of extended deterrence. Specifically, any new configuration of U.S. nuclear forces should be at least as capable in terms of its relevant attributes (such as survivability, flexibility, controllability and discrimination, and penetration capability) as the current posture. At the same time, we urge the Department to continue to conduct rigorous analysis to identify future strategic force requirements and to find cost-efficient ways to modernize the force.

VII. Strategic Risk

The growing gap between the strategic objectives the U.S. military is expected to achieve and the resources required to do so is causing risk to accumulate toward unacceptable levels. There are many tools the United States uses to reduce risk and execute its foreign and national security policy. Among these are "soft" power tools, including diplomacy, economic and trade relations, foreign aid, humanitarian assistance, and partnerships with other nations for common goals. All of these are important, but they cannot be fully effective unless they operate in concert with a robust capability to deter or defeat aggression against the United States or its allies abroad.

With regard to national security, risk is the possibility that the U.S. military may not be able to carry out some part of the national military strategy. That possibility is increasing as the global threat environment worsens, American military readiness declines, and investment in future military capabilities is cut. Without a robust, ready, and forward deployed military the United States will not long retain leadership and direction of the liberal international order so vital to American security and prosperity.

We have already discussed the increasing global threats in this period of profound strategic change and uncertainty. The bipolar constancy of the Cold War era has yielded to regional forces of instability and new strategic challenges to U.S. interests and security, as we have detailed earlier in this report. Risk is heightened as the delta between threats and capabilities grows, and that gap is expanding today. Shortfalls adding to risk include reduced capacity – the availability of forces – and reduced readiness among units required for rapid response to crisis. In addition, cuts to investment in needed future capabilities translate into additional risk in the future.

Calculation of risk is necessarily subjective and tentative because the world is unpredictable and capabilities are hard to measure on the margin. For these reasons, although both the QDR and our own recommendations stress the need for higher resource levels, there is no certainty that more defense spending alone will lower the risk of a strategy failure from high to moderate. With that caveat noted, the trend line is clear: the delta between threats and capabilities is rapidly growing. Given the uncertain global threat environment, the erosion of certain American advantages, and projected budget levels, we are prepared to say that unless recommendations of the kind we make in this report are adopted, the armed services will in the near future be at high risk of not being able to fully execute the national defense strategy. This is particularly true for the most stressing scenarios for which our forces must prepare. In the extreme, the United States could find itself in a position where it must either abandon an important national interest or enter a conflict for which it is not fully prepared.

No president should ever be forced into making such a choice. The United States can afford the armed forces it needs, and there is still time for the kind of decisive action that will lower these risks.

We do not interpret the 2014 QDR as reaching a fundamentally different conclusion than we have reached here. The QDR and the Chairman's Assessment are replete with assertions that risk will grow even if the Department receives the modest budget increases the President has requested. The QDR strongly implies, if it does not explicitly say, that under the current budget baseline of sequestration, the level of risk will rapidly become unmanageable.

APPENDICES

Appendix 1

Comparative Force Structure

Table 1 below illustrates the basic metrics of force structure since 2002. This table shows the Department's discretionary budget authority in constant 2014 dollars and the force structure the Department was able to support with that budget. Between 2002 and 2006 there was an overall reduction in force structure in Navy and Air Force while the Army and Marine Corps held their own and in fact increased slightly as a consequence of the focus on land combat power necessary to fight two difficult counterinsurgency campaigns. By 2006 both the Navy and Air Force were distinctly smaller than they were in the late 1990's – an unsettling trend the 2010 Independent Panel noted in their report. The force recommended by the 2010 QDR did not move the mark too much from the existing status quo and the 2010 Independent Panel felt it was inadequate to provide a sufficient response to a domestic catastrophe that might occur simultaneous with an ongoing overseas contingency – a very real possibility – and additionally was insufficient to address the large, increasingly-complex and maritime-centric Asia-Pacific theater. These were messages the first Independent Panel clearly communicated in its 2010 report.

The 2012 Gates Request column shows a reversal of 10-plus years of force structure erosion that Secretary Gates was determined to address. In this column, Navy is on its way to a 300-plus ship force and Air Force returns to a level of 5000-plus primary authorized aircraft. Secretary Gates intended to grow the budget by a modest, inflation-adjusted 1.8% per year which, when combined with the savings to be generated from improving the Department's business processes, would have given him the resources necessary to modernize and recapitalize the force while successfully prosecuting the wars in Iraq and Afghanistan. With the enactment of the BCA of 2011, Secretary Gates was unable to sustain the budget levels he thought necessary to rebuild the force and by 2015 the Navy, Air Force and Army had all lost capacity as indicated in the 2015 column. Possible changes in service inventory counting protocols notwithstanding, it is enlightening to compare the basic numbers in these two columns, 2012 Gates Request and 2015, and note the even deeper erosion from 2006 levels.

The QDR 2019 and Sequestration 2019 columns reflect an even bleaker picture. While the Navy's size increases by 2019 in total number of ships, they do not reach the goal of 313 ships (323 with revised Navy inventory protocols) Secretary Gates felt was necessary for a robust and sustainable U.S. forward presence, and which he targeted in his 2012 Program Acquisition Cost report. The Air Force would be reduced to a level below 1000 combat coded fighter aircraft while the Army shrinks to 56 BCT equivalents – a level that had been maintained at 70-plus since the Army undertook its initial restructuring. Under sequestration, by 2019 a further $115.2B is stripped from the President's 2015 budget request, with the deepest reductions ($35.3B and $31.4B) coming early in the FYDP years of 2016 and 2017. The effect of sequestration-level funding on force structure is truly appalling – 10 fewer ships in the Navy, 70 fewer new aircraft buys for the Air Force and the potential divestment of up to 500 legacy aircraft from its inventory, and a reduction to 46 BCT equivalents and possibly as low as 37 BCTs or roughly one-half the historical levels our Army maintained through 2012. As the End Strength section of Table 1 shows, under sequestration, total end strength could fall below 2 million service members – a floor the Department has maintained for years if not decades. The reduction in the reserve component is especially troubling in light of the increasing role we believe it will assume in future homeland defense and domestic disaster response. Table 1 clearly shows a sequestration-level force is inadequate in the face of the increasingly complex and threatening security environment we describe in our report and pales in comparison to the force structure Secretary Gates felt was the minimum essential for addressing those same security challenges.

	2002	2006	2010 QDR[a]	2012 Gates Request[b]	2015	QDR 2019 Targets	Sequestration 2019
BUDGET AUTHORITY - $B (2014 constant dollars)[1]							
Total Discretionary Budget Authority[2]	$ 447.2	$ 488.9		$ 573.6	$ 489.7	$ 524.8	$ 504.4
Military Personnel	$ 112.4	$ 123.7		$ 148.0	$ 133.3	$ 127.8	$ 127.1
Operation and Maintenance	$ 180.1	$ 177.4		$ 212.1	$ 197.7	$ 213.1	$ 206.1
Procurement[3]	$ 78.3	$ 90.1		$ 117.4	$ 88.7	$ 112.9	$ 105.7
RDT&E[4]	$ 60.6	$ 80.2		$ 78.0	$ 62.4	$ 63.2	$ 58.7
MILCON, FH, Revolving Funds	$ 15.7	$ 17.5		$ 18.2	$ 7.7	$ 7.8	$ 6.9
NAVY							
Total Ships[5]	**298**	**289**	**288 - 322**	**299**	**284**	**301**	**292**
Aircraft Carriers[6]	12	11	10 - 11	11	11	11	11
Fleet Ballistic Missile Subs (SSBN)	16	14		14	14	14	14
Guided Missile (SSGN) Subs	2	4		4	4	4	4
Nuclear Attack Subs	54	54	53 - 55	56	54	51	48
Surface Combatants[7]	106	102		116	93	110	104
Amphibious Warfare Ships[8]	38	35		31	30	32	32
Other - CLS, MW, Support, Patrol	70	69	0	67	78	79	79
AIR FORCE							
Primary Aircraft Authorized (AC + RC)[9]	**5,268**	**4,837**	**3,783**	**5,121**	**4,299**	**48 TF Sqdns**	**(500)**
Bomber	124	131	96	129	112	96	
Fighter[10]	1846	1932	1224	1469	1385	971	(21)
Trainer	1309	1036	1000	1144	1118		
AirLift[11]	754	685	1056	682	540	511	(10)
Tanker[12]	554	499		444	430	443	(17)
Other[13]	681	554	407	1253	714	307	(21)
ICBM Inventory	550	500	420	450	450	420	
LAND FORCES							
Army BCTs or BCT Equivalents (AC+RC)[14, 15]	**74**	**77**	**73**	**73**	**60**	**18 D (10/8)**	**24AC/22RC BCTs**
Heavy Brigade Combat Team (HBCT)	25	30		24	20	56 (32 AC/24 RC)	37 (18AC/19RC)
Infantry Brigade Combat Team (IBCT)	37	41		41	32		
Stryker Brigade Combat Team (SBCT)	12	6		8	8		
Marine Expeditionary Forces[16]	3	3	3	3	3	2	2
END STRENGTH (000s)							
Total Active + Reserve End strength[17]	**2,259.5**	**2,216.0**	**2,245.0**	**2,210.6**	**2,129.4**	**2,051.9**	**1,980.8**
Army AC/RC	486.5/556.6	482.4/555.0	500.0/606.0	520.0/563.2	490.0/552.2	440.0/530.0	420.0/500.0
Navy AC/RC	383.0/87.0	352.7/73.1	330.0/69.0	325.7/66.2	323.6/57.3	323.2/58.8	320.0/57.0
Marine Corps AC/RC	174.0/39.9	175.0/39.6	195.0/48.0	185.0/39.6	184.1/39.2	182.0/39.0	175.0/39.0
Air Force AC/RC	368.0/188.6	357.4/180.8	320.0/177.0	332.8/178.1	310.9/172.1	308.8/170.1	305.0/164.8

Notes on following page

1. All numbers taken from OSD Comptroller Budget Request O&M Overviews or specific Service Justification of Budget Submission documents when available. All numbers expressed in 2014 Constant dollars obtained by applying the official OSD deflators appropriate to each appropriation type for that year.

2. Service topline amounts reflect Base Budget Authority (BA) and exclude OCO and other supplementals where such figures were available and are expressed in constant 2014 dollars. QDR column reflects PB15 extended out to 2019. Sequestration column reflects 2019 amounts under BBA/BCA and are taken from DoD's 2014 Estimated Impacts of Sequestration-Level Funding report (the "Impacts" report).

3. Sequestration column: Roughly 1/3 of the cuts across the FYDP are to O&M and 2/3 are to investment (Procurement + RDT&E). O&M grows an average of 2% across the FYDP at sequestration levels vs. 3% under PB15.

4. Sequestration column: RDT&E declines across the FYDP, limiting DoD's ability to develop new technologies. Investment (Procurement + RDT&E) grows 14% under BBA/BCA levels across the FYDP vs. 23% under PB15 funding.

5. QDR column: Force numbers taken from the 2014 QDR and supplemented with information from the PB15 Shipbuilding Plan in FY19.

6. Sequestration column: Navy intends to continue to operate 11 CVNs unless CVN 68 is inactivated earlier than 2025.

7. QDR column: assumes 24 LCS, 72 DDG and 21 CG (10 in layup). Sequestration column: assumes same ship mix with loss of additional 6 DDGs in layup.

8. QDR and Sequestration column: assumes 33 total Amphibious Warfare Ships with 1 unavailable and in layup.

9. Counts are given for Primary Authorized Aircraft (PAA) not Total Aircraft Inventory (TAI). Sequestration column: Air Force 2014 Service Posture statement calls for a reduction of approximately 500 total aircraft from the combined AC/RC current inventory across the FYDP - specific types not stated.

10. QDR column: QDR states Air Force Structure as 48 fighter squadrons (26 AC / 24 RC) and a total of 971 fighter aircraft. Sequestration column: Air Force would field one fewer F-35 squadron from PB2015 levels for a reduction of 21 combat coded aircraft.

11. QDR column: Airlift and Tankers are stated as a combined figure. Sequestration column: Air Force would buy 10 fewer C-130Js.

12. Sequestration column: Air Force would buy 5 fewer KC-46As and begin an early termination of the KC-17 tanker force, resulting in 17 fewer tankers in the inventory.

13. QDR column: Only includes ISR and C2 aircraft. Counts for other airframes included in this category (e.g., Utility, Search & Rescue, R&D, etc.) were not stated. Sequestration column: Includes a reduction of at least 21 airframes including 11 Global Hawk block 40s and 10 Predator/Reapers.

14. QDR column: QDR calls for 18 Army Divisions (AC+RC). Army 2014 Service Posture statement indicates a reorganization from 38 current AC BCTs down to 32. Sequestration column: "Impacts" report indicates 24AC / 22RC BCTs. Army 2014 Service Posture statement indicates a possible decline to as few as 18AC / 19RC BCTs under sequestration

15. 2002, 2006 and 2012 columns reflect BCT equivalents during Army's shift from a Division/Battalion structure to the current Brigade Combat Team structure.

16. MEF structure has stayed constant at 3 (1 East coast, 1 West coast, 1 Asia-Pacific) since post-Korea. 2014 QDR calls for 2 MEFs to be configured from 3 AC and 1 RC Division/Wing/Log Group structure but 3 MEU command elements would remain in place where they are now geographically located.

17. Sequestration column: End strength counts either stated in the "Impacts" report or extrapolated based on mission requirements and other factors.

a. 2010 QDR force structure stated as shown in the report. The 2010 QDR proposed aggregate metrics for select elements of force structure and did not include a recommended level for each category found in this table.

b. 2012 Gates Request column shows baseline force structure inventory plus the major weapons platforms and systems included in the 2012 base Procurement Budget: Navy - 11 new ships including 2 Virginia Class SSNs, 4 LCS, 1 DDG-51, 1 LPD-17, 1 JHSV, 1 MLP and 1 Oceanographic Research Ship. Air Force - 134 new aircraft including 19 F-35s, 36 T-6B trainers, 11 C-130s, 9 C-27s and 59 ISR/C2/Utility manned and unmanned aircraft.

Appendix 2

Table 2: Impacts of Sequestration

Table 2 highlights the impact of sequestration level funding over the 2015 FYDP. It reflects the loss of $115.2B in resources from what the President Requested in his 2015 budget submission. Sequestration impacts all areas of the defense budget – Investment (Procurement plus RDT&E), Operations and Sustainment, Military Construction and Other Defense-wide Spending. Investment is especially hard hit and cuts there translate to approximately 270 fewer new weapons platforms and systems procured across the services. The table also shows the impact of a return to sequestration on investment and modernization; operational readiness (by program); facility sustainment, restoration and modernization (by service); installation services (by service); military construction; and other O&M spending, engendered by a $115.2B reduction in discretionary base estimates from the Department's planned FY15 budget levels. Almost two-thirds of this total reduction will be absorbed in Investment – Procurement plus RDT&E – needed to modernize and recapitalize our force, with the remaining roughly one-third taken from O&M accounts impacting current readiness and quality-of-life services provided to our personnel.

Item	2015	2016 ($M)	(Qty)	2017 ($M)	(Qty)	2018 ($M)	(Qty)	2019 ($M)	(Qty)	FYDP Summary ($M)	(Qty)
Procurement + RDT&E		($20,500)		($17,700)		($15,300)		($12,700)		($66,200)	
Army - Blackhawk		($334)	(15)	($821)	(42)			($85)	(4)	($1,240)	(61)
Army - Apache Remanufacture		($461)	(11)	($405)	(36)	($277)	(21)	($72)	1	($1,215)	(67)
Army - Stryker		($300)		($397)		($99)				($796)	
Army - LUH		($388)	(45)							($388)	(45)
Navy - DDG-51				($1,109)	(1)	($1,023)	(1)	($1,042)	(1)	($3,175)	(3)
Navy - Virginia Class SSN		($1,564)	(1)	$186		$161				($1,217)	(1)
Navy - Carrier Replacement		($1,385)		($349)		($543)		$1,300		($977)	
Navy - P-8A		($1,015)	(6)							($1,015)	(6)
Navy - T-AO (X)		($682)				($587)		($537)		($1,807)	
Air Force - KC-46A Tanker				($655)	(3)	($484)	(2)			($1,139)	(5)
Air Force - Combat Rescue Helo		($11)		($122)		($394)		($430)		($957)	
Air Force - MQ-9						($438)	(22)	($469)	(16)	($907)	(38)
Air Force - MC-130J		($393)	(3)	($395)	(4)	($109)	(1)	($258)	(2)	($1,155)	(10)
Air Force - GPS III		($75)		($288)	(1)	($41)				($404)	(1)
Air Force - Adaptive Engine				($155)		($506)		($670)		($1,331)	
Marine Corps - CH-53K		($41)		($426)	(2)	($267)	(2)	($301)	(3)	($1,035)	(7)
Marine Corps - ACV		($88)		($84)		($132)		($217)		($518)	
Marine Corps - V-22				$82		($133)		($269)		($320)	
Marine Corps - H-1		($111)	(4)	($57)	(2)	($60)	(2)	($88)	(3)	($315)	(11)
Joint - F-35A		($1,365)	(14)	($123)	(1)					($1,488)	(15)
Joint - F-35C		($227)	(2)							($227)	(2)
Joint - AMRAAM		($202)	(105)	($244)	(12)	($284)	(124)	($306)	(178)	($1,035)	(531)
Joint - JLTV		($46)		($44)		($436)		($60)		($585)	
Joint - JDAM		($162)	(6,860)	($165)	(6,909)		(939)		(2,390)	($327)	(17,095)
Missile Def - Interceptor Follow-on		($264)		($273)		($89)		($13)		($639)	
Missile Def - Addl Gnd-Based Sensor		($126)		($152)		($145)		($132)		($556)	
O&M - Service Readiness		($4,300)		($4,800)		($4,100)		($2,800)		($16,000)	
Army - OPTEMPO		($771)		($516)		($356)		($267)		($1,910)	
Army - Flying Hours Program		($370)		($167)		($151)		($142)		($830)	
Army - Depot Maintenance		($262)		($219)		($345)		($208)		($1,034)	
Navy - Ship Ops		($342)		($844)		($114)		($25)		($1,325)	
Navy & MC - Flying Hours Program		($307)		($299)		($275)		($321)		($1,202)	
Navy - Ship Maintenance		($251)		($312)		($562)		($377)		($1,502)	
Navy & MC - Aviation Depot Maint		($57)		($109)		($66)		($94)		($325)	
Air Force - Flying Hours Program		($167)		($182)		($185)		($167)		($701)	
Air Force - Aviation Depot Maint		($1,572)		($2,028)		($1,873)		($1,037)		($6,510)	
Marine Corps - Operating Forces		($81)		($94)		($87)		($102)		($364)	
Marine Corps - Depot Maint		($95)		($68)		($60)		($90)		($313)	
O&M - FSRM		($1,900)		($2,000)		($1,800)		($1,300)		($7,000)	
Army		($390)		($598)		($685)		($593)		($2,266)	
Navy		($644)		($563)		($427)		($447)		($2,081)	
Air Force		($695)		($602)		($488)		($190)		($1,940)	
Marine Corps		($220)		($202)		($175)		($107)		($704)	
O&M - Installation Services		($1,800)		($1,200)		($1,000)		($800)		($4,800)	
Army		($1,573)		($960)		($709)		($572)		($3,813)	
Navy		($57)		($52)		($53)		($53)		($215)	
Air Force		$23		($25)		($25)		($26)		($52)	
Marine Corps		($166)		($177)		($182)		($186)		($711)	
O&M - Non-Defense and All Other O&M		($4,100)		($3,279)		($2,549)		($2,394)		($12,322)	
MILCON - All Services		($2,000)		($1,600)		($1,100)		($900)		($5,700)	
Other Defense-wide		($700)		($810)		($760)		($1,005)		($3,180)	
Total Reductions		($35,300)		($31,389)		($26,609)		($21,899)		($115,202)	

All dollar values represent the delta between PB15 amounts and amounts under BBA/BCA Sequestration level funding. Quanties expressed in number of units planned for procurement under PB15 but NOT procured due to sequestration-level funding. In 2015, PB15 and BBA/BCA amounts are identical - no deltas exist.

Appendix 3

Glossary

A2AD	anti-access and area-denial
AVF	All-Volunteer Force
BCA	Budget Control Act
BRAC	Base Realignment and Closure
BUR	Bottom-Up Review
CBO	Congressional Budget Office
DOD	Department of Defense
FY	Fiscal Year
FYDP	Future Year Defense Program
ISR	intelligence, surveillance and reconnaissance
MILSATCOM	Military Satellite Communications Systems Directorate
NATO	North Atlantic Treaty Organization
ONR	Office of Naval Research
PLA	People's Liberation Army
QDR	Quadrennial Defense Review
RIF	Reduction in Force
ROK	Republic of Korea
SSGN	nuclear-guided missile submarine
SSN	nuclear-powered attack submarine
START	Strategic Arms Reduction Treaty
UUV	unmanned undersea vehicle
VSIP	Voluntary Separation Incentive Payment
WMD	weapons of mass destruction
WTO	World Trade Organization

Appendix 4

Enabling Legislation

10 U.S.C. § 118: US Code – Section 118: Quadrennial Defense Review

(a) Review Required.-The Secretary of Defense shall every four years, during a year following a year evenly divisible by four, conduct a comprehensive examination (to be known as a "quadrennial defense review") of the national defense strategy, force structure, force modernization plans, infrastructure, budget plan, and other elements of the defense program and policies of the United States with a view toward determining and expressing the defense strategy of the United States and establishing a defense program for the next 20 years. Each such quadrennial defense review shall be conducted in consultation with the Chairman of the Joint Chiefs of Staff.

(b) Conduct of Review.-Each quadrennial defense review shall be conducted so as-

(1) to delineate a national defense strategy consistent with the most recent National Security Strategy prescribed by the President pursuant to section 108 of the National Security Act of 1947 (50 U.S.C. 404a); [1]

(2) to define sufficient force structure, force modernization plans, infrastructure, budget plan, and other elements of the defense program of the United States associated with that national defense strategy that would be required to execute successfully the full range of missions called for in that national defense strategy;

(3) to identify (A) the budget plan that would be required to provide sufficient resources to execute successfully the full range of missions called for in that national defense strategy at a low-to-moderate level of risk, and (B) any additional resources (beyond those programmed in the current future-years defense program) required to achieve such a level of risk; and

(4) to make recommendations that are not constrained to comply with and are fully independent of the budget submitted to Congress by the President pursuant to section 1105 of title 31.

(c) Assessment of Risk.-The assessment of risk for the purposes of subsection (b) shall be undertaken by the Secretary of Defense in consultation with the Chairman of the Joint Chiefs of Staff. That assessment shall define the nature and magnitude of the political, strategic, and military risks associated with executing the missions called for under the national defense strategy.

(d) Submission of QDR to Congressional Committees.-The Secretary shall submit a report on each quadrennial defense review to the Committees on Armed Services of the Senate and the House of Representatives. The report shall be submitted in the year following the year in which the review is conducted, but not later than the date on which the President submits the budget for the next fiscal year to Congress under section 1105(a) of title 31. The report shall include the following:

(1) The results of the review, including a comprehensive discussion of the national defense strategy of the United States, the strategic planning guidance, and the force structure best suited to implement that strategy at a low-to-moderate level of risk.

(2) The assumed or defined national security interests of the United States that inform the national defense strategy defined in the review.

(3) The threats to the assumed or defined national security interests of the United States that were examined for the purposes of the review and the scenarios developed in the examination of those threats.

(4) The assumptions used in the review, including assumptions relating to-

    (A) the status of readiness of United States forces;

    (B) the cooperation of allies, mission-sharing and additional benefits to and burdens on United States forces resulting from coalition operations;

    (C) warning times;

    (D) levels of engagement in operations other than war and smaller-scale contingencies and withdrawal from such operations and contingencies;

    (E) the intensity, duration, and military and political end-states of conflicts and smaller-scale contingencies; and

    (F) the roles and responsibilities that would be discharged by contractors.

(5) The effect on the force structure and on readiness for high-intensity combat of preparations for and participation in operations other than war and smaller-scale contingencies.

(6) The manpower, sustainment, and contractor support policies required under the national defense strategy to support engagement in conflicts lasting longer than 120 days.

(7) The anticipated roles and missions of the reserve components in the national defense strategy and the strength, capabilities, and equipment necessary to assure that the reserve components can capably discharge those roles and missions.

(8) The appropriate ratio of combat forces to support forces (commonly referred to as the "tooth-to-tail" ratio) under the national defense strategy, including, in particular, the appropriate number and size of headquarters units and Defense Agencies, and the scope of contractor support, for that purpose.

(9) The specific capabilities, including the general number and type of specific military platforms, needed to achieve the strategic and warfighting objectives identified in the review.

(10) The strategic and tactical air-lift, sea-lift, and ground transportation capabilities required to support the national defense strategy.

(11) The forward presence, pre-positioning, and other anticipatory deployments necessary under the national defense strategy for conflict deterrence and adequate military response to anticipated conflicts.

(12) The extent to which resources must be shifted among two or more theaters under the national defense strategy in the event of conflict in such theaters.

(13) The advisability of revisions to the Unified Command Plan as a result of the national defense strategy.

(14) The effect on force structure of the use by the armed forces of technologies anticipated to be available for the ensuing 20 years.

(15) The national defense mission of the Coast Guard.

(16) The homeland defense and support to civil authority missions of the active and reserve components, including the organization and capabilities required for the active and reserve components to discharge each such mission.

(17) Any other matter the Secretary considers appropriate.

(e) *CJCS Review.-*

(1) Upon the completion of each review under subsection (a), the Chairman of the Joint Chiefs of Staff shall prepare and submit to the Secretary of Defense the Chairman's assessment of the review, including the Chairman's assessment of risk and a description of the capabilities needed to address such risk.

(2) The Chairman's assessment shall be submitted to the Secretary in time for the inclusion of the assessment in the report. The Secretary shall include the Chairman's assessment, together with the Secretary's comments, in the report in its entirety.

(f) *National Defense Panel.-*

(1) Establishment.-Not later than February 1 of a year in which a quadrennial defense review is conducted under this section, there shall be established an independent panel to be known as the National Defense Panel (in this subsection referred to as the "Panel"). The Panel shall have the duties set forth in this subsection.

(2) Membership.-The Panel shall be composed of ten members from private civilian life who are recognized experts in matters relating to the national security of the United States. Eight of the members shall be appointed as follows:

(A) Two by the chairman of the Committee on Armed Services of the House of Representatives.

(B) Two by the chairman of the Committee on Armed Services of the Senate.

(C) Two by the ranking member of the Committee on Armed Services of the House of Representatives.

(D) Two by the ranking member of the Committee on Armed Services of the Senate.

(3) Co-chairs of the panel.-In addition to the members appointed under paragraph (2), the Secretary of Defense shall appoint two members from private civilian life to serve as co-chairs of the panel.

(4) Period of appointment; vacancies.-Members shall be appointed for the life of the Panel. Any vacancy in the Panel shall be filled in the same manner as the original appointment.

(5) Duties.-The Panel shall have the following duties with respect to a quadrennial defense review:

(A) While the review is being conducted, the Panel shall review the updates from the Secretary of Defense required under paragraph (8) on the conduct of the review.

(B) The Panel shall-

(i) review the Secretary of Defense's terms of reference and any other materials providing the basis for, or substantial inputs to, the work of the Department of Defense on the quadrennial defense review;

(ii) conduct an assessment of the assumptions, strategy, findings, and risks of the report on the quadrennial defense review required in subsection (d), with particular attention paid to the risks described in that report;

(iii) conduct an independent assessment of a variety of possible force structures of the armed forces, including the force structure identified in the report on the quadrennial defense review required in subsection (d);

(iv) review the resource requirements identified pursuant to subsection (b)(3) and, to the extent practicable, make a general comparison to the resource requirements to support the forces contemplated under the force structures assessed under this subparagraph; and

(v) provide to Congress and the Secretary of Defense, through the report under paragraph (7), any recommendations it considers appropriate for their consideration.

(6) First meeting.-If the Secretary of Defense has not made the Secretary's appointments to the Panel under paragraph (3) by February 1 of a year in which a quadrennial defense review is conducted under this section, the Panel shall convene for its first meeting with the remaining members.

(7) Report.-Not later than 3 months after the date on which the report on a quadrennial defense review is submitted under subsection (d) to the congressional committees named in that subsection, the Panel established under paragraph (1) shall submit to those committees

an assessment of the quadrennial defense review, including a description of the items addressed under paragraph (5) with respect to that quadrennial defense review.

(8) Updates from secretary of defense.-The Secretary of Defense shall ensure that periodically, but not less often than every 60 days, or at the request of the co-chairs, the Department of Defense briefs the Panel on the progress of the conduct of a quadrennial defense review under subsection (a).

(9) Administrative provisions.-

(A) The Panel may request directly from the Department of Defense and any of its components such information as the Panel considers necessary to carry out its duties under this subsection. The head of the department or agency concerned shall cooperate with the Panel to ensure that information requested by the Panel under this paragraph is promptly provided to the maximum extent practical.

(B) Upon the request of the co-chairs, the Secretary of Defense shall make available to the Panel the services of any federally funded research and development center that is covered by a sponsoring agreement of the Department of Defense.

(C) The Panel shall have the authorities provided in section 3161 of title 5 and shall be subject to the conditions set forth in such section.

(D) Funds for activities of the Panel shall be provided from amounts available to the Department of Defense.

(10) Termination.-The Panel for a quadrennial defense review shall terminate 45 days after the date on which the Panel submits its final report on the quadrennial defense review under paragraph (7).

(g) *Consideration of Effect of Climate Change on Department Facilities, Capabilities, and Missions.-*

(1) The first national security strategy and national defense strategy prepared after January 28, 2008, shall include guidance for military planners-

(A) to assess the risks of projected climate change to current and future missions of the armed forces;

(B) to update defense plans based on these assessments, including working with allies and partners to incorporate climate mitigation strategies, capacity building, and relevant research and development; and

(C) to develop the capabilities needed to reduce future impacts.

(2) The first quadrennial defense review prepared after January 28, 2008, shall also examine the capabilities of the armed forces to respond to the consequences of climate change, in particular, preparedness for natural disasters from extreme weather events and other missions the armed forces may be asked to support inside the United States and overseas.

(3) For planning purposes to comply with the requirements of this subsection, the Secretary of Defense shall use-

(A) the mid-range projections of the fourth assessment report of the Intergovernmental Panel on Climate Change;

(B) subsequent mid-range consensus climate projections if more recent information is available when the next national security strategy, national defense strategy, or quadrennial defense review, as the case may be, is conducted; and

(C) findings of appropriate and available estimations or studies of the anticipated strategic, social, political, and economic effects of global climate change and the implications of such effects on the national security of the United States.

(4) In this subsection, the term "national security strategy" means the annual national security strategy report of the President under section 108 of the National Security Act of 1947 (50 U.S.C. 404a).[1]

(h) *Relationship to Budget.-Nothing in this section shall be construed to affect section 1105(a) of title 31.*

(i) *Interagency Overseas Basing Report.-(*1) Not later than 90 days after submitting a report on a quadrennial defense review under subsection (d), the Secretary of Defense shall submit to the congressional defense committees a report detailing how the results of the assessment conducted as part of such review will impact-

(A) the status of overseas base closure and realignment actions undertaken as part of a global defense posture realignment strategy; and

(B) the status of development and execution of comprehensive master plans for overseas military main operating bases, forward operating sites, and cooperative security locations of the global defense posture of the United States.

(2) A report under paragraph (1) shall include any recommendations for additional closures or realignments of military installations outside of the United States and any comments resulting from an interagency review of these plans that includes the Department of State and other relevant Federal departments and agencies.

Appendix 5

National Defense Panel Plenary Schedule

August 20, 2013

September 24, 2013

October 29, 2013

December 3, 2013

January 14, 2014

February 28, 2014

March 28, 2014

April 22, 2014

May 7, 2014

Appendix 6
Consultations

Current U.S. Administration Officials

Civilian:

Jeri Busch	*Director, Military Compensation, Personnel and Readiness (P&R)*
Dan Chiu	*Deputy Assistant Secretary for Strategy*
Scott A. Comes	*Deputy Director for Program Evaluation, Cost Assessment and Program Evaluation (CAPE)*
John Conger	*Acting Deputy Under Secretary of Defense for Installations & Environment (AT&L)*
Lisa Disbrow	*Vice Director for Force Structure, Resources, and Assessment, Joint Staff, J-8*
James Fasano	*Budget Analyst, Military Personnel & Construction Directorate, Office of the Under Secretary of Defense, Comptroller (C)*
Charles "Chuck" Hagel	*Secretary of Defense*
Mara Karlin	*Principal Director for Strategy, Policy (P)*
James Miller	*Under Secretary for Defense, (P)*
Joe Nogueira	*Deputy Director, Program Data and Enterprise Services, Office of the Under Secretary of Defense (CAPE)*
David Ochmanek	*Deputy Assistant Secretary of Defense for Force Development*
Robert Opsut	*Office of the Assistant Secretary of Defense (Health Affairs)*
Eric Rosenbach	*Deputy Assistant Secretary of Defense for Cyber Policy*
Mathew Schaffer	*Deputy Director, Office of the Undersecretary of Defense (CAPE)*

Robert Scher	*Deputy Assistant Secretary of Defense for South and Southeast Asia*
Chris Smith	*Budget Analyst, Military Personnel & Construction Directorate, Office of the Under Secretary of Defense (C)*
JP Wilusz	*Division Director, Office of the Undersecretary of Defense (CAPE)*
Christine Wormuth	*Deputy Under Secretary of Defense for Strategy, Plans and Force Development*

Military:

General James Amos	*Commandant, U.S. Marine Corps*
General Lloyd Austin	*Commander, U.S. Central Command (CENTCOM)*
Arthur H Barber, III	*Deputy Director, Assessments Division, N81, Office of the Chief of Naval Operations (OPNAV)*
Rear Admiral Ronald A. Boxall, USN	*Deputy Director, Joint Strategic Planning, J5, Joint Staff*
Brigadier General Courtney Carr	*Deputy Director of Operations, Readiness and Mobilization*
Rear Admiral Peter J. Fanta, USN	*Deputy Director for Resources and Acquisition, Joint Staff*
Admiral Jonathon Greenert	*Chief of Naval Operations, U.S. Navy*
Lieutenant General Bradley Heithold	*Vice Commander, U.S. Special Operations Command (SOCOM)*
Major General Steven Kwast	*Commander, Curtis E. LeMay Center for Doctrine Development and Education, U.S. Air Force*
Lieutenant General Robert Lennox	*PD Director, Office of the Undersecretary of Defense (CAPE)*
General Raymond "Ray" Odierno	*Chief of Staff, U.S. Army*
Rear Admiral Herman A. Shelanski	*Director, Assessment Division, N81, OPNAV*
General Larry Spencer	*Vice Chief of Staff, U.S. Air Force*
Admiral James "Sandy" Winnefeld	*Vice Chairman, Joint Chiefs of Staff*

National Intelligence Council

Daniel Flynn	*Director, Global Security Program in the Strategic Futures Group*
John D. Williams	*National Intelligence Officer for Military Issues*

Military Veterans Service Organizations

Kathy Beasley	*Military Officers Association of America*
Andrew Davis	*Reserve Officers Association*
Marshall Hanson	*Reserve Officers Association*
Mike Hayden	*Military Officers Association of America*
James Offutt	*Navy League of the United States*
John Stovall	*American Legion*
Guy Swan	*Association of the United States Army*

Other Experts

Gordon Adams	*Stimson Center*
Sam Brennan	*Center for Strategic and International Studies*
Shawn Brimley	*Center for a New American Security*
Kurt Campbell	*Center for a New American Security*
Thomas Donnelly	*AEI*
Karl Eikenberry	*Stanford University*
Roy Evans, JR	*The MITRE Corporation*
Todd Harris	*CSBA*
James Hartneady, JR	*The MITRE Corporation*
George Henes	*First Secretary, Defense Policy and Strategy, British Embassy*
Francis Hedley Robertson "Buster" Howes	*Defense Attaché, British Embassy*
Will Jessett	*Minister for Defense Material, UK MOD*
Andrew Krepinevich	*CSBA*

Alphonso Maldon, JR	*Chairman, Military Compensation and Retirement Modernization Commission*
Frank Miller	*Strategic Studies Institute, United States Army War College*
Barry Pavel	*Atlantic Council*
Robert Work	*Center for a New American Security*
Larry Wortzel	*Representative, U.S. China Commission*

Appendix 7

QDR National Defense Panel Member Biographies

William J. Perry—Co-Chairman

William Perry is the Michael and Barbara Berberian Professor (emeritus) at Stanford University. He is a senior fellow at FSI and serves as co-director of the Nuclear Risk Reduction initiative and the Preventive Defense Project. He is an expert in U.S. foreign policy, national security and arms control. He was the co-director of CISAC from 1988 to 1993, during which time he was also a professor (half time) at Stanford. He was a part-time lecturer in the Department of Mathematics at Santa Clara University from 1971 to 1977.

Perry was the 19th secretary of defense for the United States, serving from February 1994 to January 1997. He previously served as deputy secretary of defense (1993-1994) and as under secretary of defense for research and engineering (1977-1981). Dr. Perry currently serves on the Defense Policy Board (DPB) and International Security Advisory Board (ISAB) and Nuclear Defense Policy (NDP) board. He is on the board of directors of CoVant Technologies, Fabrinet, USA, LGS Bell Labs Innovations and several emerging high-tech companies. His previous business experience includes serving as a laboratory director for General Telephone and Electronics (1954-1964); founder and president of ESL Inc. (1964-1977); executive vice-president of Hambrecht & Quist Inc. (1981-1985); and founder and chairman of Technology Strategies & Alliances (1985-1993). He is a member of the National Academy of Engineering and a fellow of the American Academy of Arts and Sciences.

From 1946 to 1947, Perry was an enlisted man in the Army Corps of Engineers, and served in the Army of Occupation in Japan. He joined the Reserve Officer Training Corps in 1948 and was a second lieutenant in the Army Reserves from 1950 to 1955. He was awarded the Presidential Medal of Freedom in 1997 and The Knight Commander of the British Empire in 1998. Perry has received a number of other awards including the Department of Defense Distinguished Service Medal (1980 and 1981), and Outstanding Civilian Service Medals from the Army (1962 and 1997), the Air Force (1997), the Navy (1997), the Defense Intelligence Agency (1977 and 1997), NASA (1981) and the Coast Guard (1997). He received the American Electronic Association's Medal of Achievement (1980), the Eisenhower Award (1996), the Marshall Award (1997), the Forrestal Medal (1994), and the Henry Stimson Medal (1994). The National Academy of Engineering selected him for the Arthur Bueche Medal in 1996. He has received awards from the enlisted personnel of the Army, Navy, and the Air Force. He has received decorations from the governments of Albania, Bahrain, France, Germany, Hungary, Japan, Korea, Poland, Slovenia, and Ukraine. He received a BS and MS from Stanford University and a PhD from Pennsylvania State University, all in mathematics.

John P. Abizaid—Co-Chairman

John P. Abizaid retired from the United States Army in May, 2007, after thirty-four years of active service. After graduating from the United States Military Academy at West Point, he rose from second lieutenant of infantry to four-star general in the Army. At the time of his retirement he was the longest-serving commander of United States Central Command, with responsibility for an area spanning 27 countries in the Middle East, Southwest Asia, and the Horn of Africa. During a distinguished career he commanded units at every level, serving in the combat zones of Grenada, Lebanon, Kurdistan, Bosnia, Kosovo, Afghanistan and Iraq. Units under his command have included the 1st Infantry Division, a brigade in the 82nd Airborne Division, and two Ranger companies. Abizaid worked on the Joint Staff three times, the last as Director. He studied at the University of Jordan in Amman, holds a master's degree in Middle Eastern Studies from Harvard University, and is widely considered to be an expert in the field of Middle Eastern affairs.

Through his consulting company, JPA Partners LLC, General Abizaid advises small businesses through Fortune 500 companies nationally and internationally on leadership, security, and management issues. He serves as a Board Member for both USAA and RPM, Inc. General Abizaid also supports and advises the Combating Terrorism Center at West Point, as well as several other charity and non-profit organizations and foundations.

James Cartwright—Member

General James Cartwright retired from active duty on 1 September 2011, after 40 years of service in the United States Marine Corps.

Unique among Marines, General Cartwright served as Commander, U.S. Strategic Command, before being nominated and appointed as the 8th Vice Chairman of the Joint Chiefs of Staff, the nation's second highest military officer. General Cartwright served his four year tenure as Vice Chairman across two Presidential administrations and constant military operations against diverse and evolving enemies. He became widely recognized for his technical acumen, vision of future national security concepts, and keen ability to integrate systems, organizations and people in ways that encouraged creativity and sparked innovation in the areas of strategic deterrence, nuclear proliferation, missile defense, cyber security, and adaptive acquisition processes.

Born in Rockford, IL, he attended the University of Iowa and was commissioned a Second Lieutenant of Marines in 1971. He was both a Naval Flight Officer and Naval Aviator who flew the F-4 Phantom, OA-4 Skyhawk, and F/A-18 Hornet. In 1983 he was named Outstanding Carrier Aviator of the Year by the Association of Naval Aviation. General Cartwright graduated with distinction from the Air Command and Staff College, received a Master of Arts in National Security and Strategic Studies from the Naval War College, completed a fellowship with the Massachusetts Institute of Technology, and was honored with a Naval War College Distinguished Graduate Leadership Award.

General Cartwright currently serves as the inaugural holder of the Harold Brown Chair in Defense Policy Studies for the Center for Strategic & International Studies. In addition, General Cartwright serves as a member of The Raytheon Company Board of Directors, a Harvard Belfer Center Senior Fellow, and a defense consultant for ABC News.

General Cartwright is also an advisor for several corporate entities involved in global management consulting; technology services and program solutions; predictive and Big Data Analytics; and advanced systems engineering, integration, and decision-support services. He serves as an advisor to the Boards of Directors for Accenture Federal Services, Enlightenment Capital, IxReveal, HSH Analytics, Logos Technologies, Opera Solutions, and TASC. General Cartwright is also affiliated with a number of professional organizations to include the Aspen Strategy Group, The Atlantic Council, Global Zero, and the Nuclear Threat Initiative.

Eric S. Edelman—Member

Ambassador Eric S. Edelman retired as a Career Minister from the U.S. Foreign Service on May 1, 2009. He is currently the Hertog Distinguished Practitioner in Residence at the Philip Merrill Center for Strategic Studies at the Johns Hopkins University School of Advanced International Studies and a Distinguished Fellow at the Center for Strategic and Budgetary Assessments. He was a senior associate of the International Security Program at the Belfer Center for Science and International Affairs at Harvard University from 2009-2013. He is also a member of the Board of Directors of the United States Institute of Peace.

Ambassador Edelman has served in senior positions at the Departments of State and Defense as well as the White House where he led organizations providing analysis, strategy, policy development, security services, trade advocacy, public outreach, citizen services and congressional relations. As the Under Secretary of Defense for Policy (August, 2005-January 2009) he oversaw strategy development as DoD's senior policy official with global responsibility for bilateral defense relations, war plans, special operations forces, homeland defense, missile defense, nuclear weapons and arms control policies, counter-proliferation, counter-narcotics, counter-terrorism, arms sales, and defense trade controls.

He served as U.S. Ambassador to the Republics of Finland and Turkey in the Clinton and Bush Administrations and was Principal Deputy Assistant to the Vice President for National Security Affairs. In other assignment he has been Chief of Staff to Deputy Secretary of State Strobe Talbott, special assistant to Under Secretary of State for Political Affairs Robert Kimmitt and special assistant to Secretary of State George Shultz. His other assignments include the State Department Operations Center, Prague, Moscow, and Tel Aviv, where he was a member of the U.S. Middle East Delegation to the West Bank/Gaza Autonomy Talks.

He has been awarded the Department of Defense Medal for Distinguished Public Service, the Presidential Distinguished Service Award, and several Department of State Superior Honor Awards. In January 2011 he was awarded the Legion d'Honneur by the French Government.

He received a B.A. in History and Government from Cornell University and a Ph.D. in U.S. Diplomatic History from Yale University.

Michèle Flournoy—Member

Michèle Flournoy is Co-Founder and CEO of the Center for a New American Security and a Senior Advisor at the Boston Consulting Group.

From 2009 to 2012, she served as the Under Secretary of Defense for Policy, the principal adviser to the Secretary of Defense in the formulation of national security and defense policy, oversight of military plans and operations, and in National Security Council deliberations. She led the development of DoD's FY2013 Strategic Guidance and represented the Department in dozens of foreign engagements, in the media and before Congress.

After the 2008 election, Ms. Flournoy co-led President Obama's transition team at DoD.

In January 2007, Ms. Flournoy co-founded the Center for a New American Security (CNAS), a non-partisan think tank dedicated to developing strong, pragmatic and principled national security policies, and served as CNAS' President.

Previously, she was senior adviser at the Center for Strategic and International Studies and, prior to that, a distinguished research professor at the Institute for National Strategic Studies at the National Defense University (NDU).

In the mid-1990s, she served as Principal Deputy Assistant Secretary of Defense for Strategy and Threat Reduction and Deputy Assistant Secretary of Defense for Strategy in the Clinton administration.

She received the Department of Defense Medal for Distinguished Public Service in 1998, 2011, and 2012, the Chairman of the Joint Chiefs of Staff's Joint Distinguished Civilian Service Award in 2000 and 2012, and the Secretary of Defense Medal for Outstanding Public Service in 1996.

She is a frequent commentator in the media, has edited several books and written dozens of reports and articles on a broad range of defense and national security issues

She now serves on several boards and is also a Senior Fellow at Harvard's Belfer Center for Science and International Affairs and a member of the Defense Policy Board, the DCIA's External Advisory Board, the Aspen Strategy Group, and the Council on Foreign Relations.

She earned her B.A. from Harvard University and her Masters in International Relations from Balliol College, Oxford University, where she was a Newton-Tatum Scholar.

Francis (Frank) H. Kearney III—Member

Lieutenant General Frank Kearney retired on 1 January 2012 from the United States Army after more than 35 years of service. His final active duty assignment was Deputy Director for Strategic Operational Planning at the National Counter-Terrorism Center in Washington DC. General Kearney now serves as the President of his own consulting company, Inside-Solutions-LLC focusing on leader development in organizations and is a partner in and co-founder of Willowdale Services LLC, which invests in and develops small businesses, performs national security consulting, as well as leader development training and mentoring. He works routinely with the Thayer Leader Development Group at the Thayer Hotel at West Point, NY and with military and corporate groups to assist in improving organizational performance through leader development. In this capacity he has worked with leaders in 7-11, Deloitte, General Electric, USAA, Novartis, Madison Square Garden, China-Europe International Business School and many others. General Kearney serves as the Chairman of the Advisory Board for Team Red, White and Blue, a non-profit that helps reintegrate wounded warriors into their communities through physical and social activities, as well as on the advisory boards for the Thayer Leader Development Group, Red Gate Group, Xtreme Precision Firearms, Tiger Swan International, Reperi and Teradact Solutions. General Kearney is a routine speaker on Terrorism, Interagency, Defense and Security issues. General Kearney continues to serve as a member of the Threat Reduction Advisory Committee (TRAC) to the Secretary of Defense. General Kearney also serves as a mentor with the Department of State Foreign Service Institute's National Senior Executive Leadership Seminar.

General Kearney is a 1976 graduate (BS) of the United States Military Academy and a 1985 graduate (MEd) of the University of South Carolina. He is a graduate of the US Army Command and General Staff College as well as the United States Army War College. He has served in operational and command assignments at every level with combat tours in Grenada, Panama, Bosnia, Iraq and Afghanistan. General Kearney's most recent assignments at the strategic and operational level focused on Special Operations and Counter-Terrorism. He planned and participated in the opening campaigns of Operation Enduring Freedom in Afghanistan and Operation Iraqi Freedom in Iraq and commanded all Theater Special Operations forces in the middle-east including OIF and OEF from March 2005 to June 2007. General Kearney also served as the Deputy Combatant Commander for United States Special Operations Command (SOCOM) from 2007-2010 and insured that the 62,000 operators of this command were properly trained and equipped for their global special operation's missions. General Kearney oversaw the SOCOM requirements process, the execution of a 9 billion dollar budget and led the SOCOM Quadrennial Defense Review (QDR) team for the 2010 QDR. General Kearney also sat on the DOD Ballistic Missile Defense Review Committee and the Deputy Secretary of Defense's Advisory Working Group managing the Department's annual budget approval and execution. Finally, at the National Counter-Terrorism Center, General Kearney worked with 16-29 different cabinet level agencies in the US government to plan and coordinate the whole of government efforts to achieve the goals of the Obama Administration's Counter-Terrorism strategy. His team coordinated key implementation plans against terrorist groups and assessed the efforts to achieve stated goals as well as provided input to the Office of Management and Budget on funding priorities for the national counter-terrorism budget.

LTG Kearney's family includes his wife of 37 years, Betty Sue, their son Major Dan Kearney, his wife Lauren and sons Danny (6) and Jack (3). Sean Kearney, a CPA with Price-Waterhouse-Coopers, resides in Charlotte, NC.

Michael D. Maples—Member

Lieutenant General Maples retired from the United States Army in 2009 with over 37 years of service. In his final assignment, he served as the Director of the Defense Intelligence Agency (DIA) (2005-2009) and simultaneously as the Commander of the Joint Functional Component Command for Intelligence, Surveillance and Reconnaissance (JFCC-ISR) for U.S. Strategic Command.

Following graduation from the United States Military Academy in 1971, Mike served as a Field Artillery officer, commanding a nuclear capable firing battery in the Republic of Korea, a Multiple Launch Rocket System (MLRS) battalion during combat in Operations Desert Shield/Desert Storm, and the last U.S. Army Field Artillery Brigade forward deployed in Germany. He was the Commanding General of the United States Army Field Artillery Center and Fort Sill.

He participated in Operation Joint Endeavor while serving in Germany and Hungary. As the Deputy Chief of Staff for Operations and Intelligence of NATO's Allied Rapid Reaction Corps and Kosovo Force he coordinated the initial entry of NATO forces into Macedonia and Kosovo during Operation Joint Guardian.

LTG (R) Maples had three Pentagon assignments including Vice Director of the Joint Staff and Director of Operations, Readiness and Mobilization on the Army Staff.

He is currently engaged in a range of business activities and personal interests, including participation in the Elbe Group, a forum sponsored by the Belfer Center at Harvard University, whose members maintain an open and continuous channel of communication on issues related to US-Russian relations with a primary focus on reducing the threat of nuclear terrorism.

Jim Marshall—Member

Congressman Jim Marshall (2003–2011) is the immediate past President of the United States Institute of Peace where he served from 2012-2014. He is a business lawyer and law professor, former mayor of Macon, Georgia and member of the United States Army Ranger Hall of Fame. He serves on the board of the National Futures Association and taught at Princeton University's

Woodrow Wilson School of Public and International Affairs during 2011 and 2012. His courses at Princeton focused upon the limited utility of American military force.

In Congress Jim served on the Armed Services, Agriculture, and Financial Services committees. His Armed Services subcommittees were Readiness and Terrorism, Unconventional Threats and Capabilities. He chaired the Air Force Caucus, the Financial Markets Caucus, the Balanced Budget Caucus and West Point's Board of Visitors. As mayor of Macon, Jim served on the Advisory Board of the United States Conference of Mayors and co-chaired the National Conference of Democratic Mayors.

After the Tet Offensive in 1968, Jim withdrew from Princeton University to volunteer for Vietnam where he served in ground combat as an Airborne Ranger reconnaissance platoon sergeant. He has received numerous military awards and recognitions, including the Purple Heart and membership in the United States Army Ranger Hall of Fame.

After his tour in Vietnam, Jim returned to Princeton where he was a University Scholar and graduated in 1972. He received a JD from Boston University School of Law in 1977, finishing second in his class. After clerking for two federal district court judges, Jim joined the law faculty at Mercer University in 1979. In addition to numerous civic roles, for the next sixteen years before becoming Mayor of Macon, Jim taught, wrote about, and actively practiced business law, representing companies, financial institutions and individuals in commercial, insolvency, property, and financial matters.

Gregory S. Martin—Member

General Gregory S. Martin retired from the United States Air Force in September 2005 as the Commander of the Air Force Materiel Command after having served thirty-five years on active duty.

After graduating from the United States Air Force Academy in 1970 and pilot training in 1971, General Martin began his career as a fighter pilot with a combat tour in Southeast Asia. Over the next twenty years he served in a variety of staff and flying assignments which led to his selection as fighter wing commander on three successive assignments. For the remainder of his career, General Martin served in senior level staff assignments on the Joint Staff, the Air Staff and the Secretariat of the Air Force before being selected as the Commander of United States Air Forces Europe and Commander of NATO's Allied Air Forces Northern Europe. While in Europe, General Martin commanded joint and combined air forces supporting and participating in Operations Northern Watch over northern Iraq, Operations Joint Forge and Joint Guardian in Bosnia and Kosovo, Operations Enduring Freedom in Afghanistan and Operation Iraqi Freedom in Iraq.

In his final assignment, General Martin commanded nearly 80,000 military and civilian personnel responsible for: The Air Force's Science and Technology programs executed through the Air Force Research Laboratory; all personnel and infrastructure required to support the Assistant Secretary of the Air Force for Acquisition's management of all aircraft, munitions, and command, control, communications and computer system acquisition programs; the Air Force's Developmental Test and Evaluation activities; and the Air Force's logistics, engineering and depot maintenance operations. The Air Force Materiel Command is responsible for executing nearly $40 Billion per year, or approximately half of the Air Force's annual budget.

Since retiring from the Air Force, General Martin has become an independent consultant. He serves as the Chair of the Board of Directors for the National Academies' Air Force Studies Board and performs mentoring duties as a Highly Qualified Expert for the Joint Staff in the Department of Defense. He has served as a committee member on two Defense Science Board task force studies. Additionally, he serves on several advisory boards and as a consultant for a number of defense and aerospace industry corporations. He is also the Chairman of the Falcon Foundation, which provides scholarship funding for promising young men and women aspiring to attend the United States Air Force Academy.

James Talent—Member

Jim Talent served the people of Missouri for 20 years in the State Legislature, the United States House of Representatives, and the United States Senate. During his years in Congress, he was an advocate for a strong national defense. He formed an "Ad-Hoc Committee on the Hollowing of the Armed Forces" and spoke out on the House floor against the cuts in the size and strength of the military in the immediate aftermath of the Cold War. He continued these efforts during eight years in the House on the Senate Armed Services Committee and then again in the Senate on the Senate Armed Services Committee, where he was Chairman of the Naval Power Subcommittee. His last speech in the Senate in 2006 was on the need to rebuild the armed services. Since leaving the Senate, Senator Talent has continued his national security work. He is a Distinguished Fellow at the Heritage Foundation specializing in military affairs. He served as the Co-Chairman of the Graham/Talent Commission on Weapons of Mass Destruction Proliferation and Terrorism. He was a member of the Perry/Hadley Commission which reviewed the Department of Defense's Quadrennial Defense Review in 2010. In 2013, Senator Mitch McConnell appointed Senator Talent to the U.S. China Economic and Security Review Commission, a standing Commission that reports to Congress every year on the relationship between the United States and China.

Senator Talent was the senior advisor to Governor Mitt Romney on matters relating to the military in both the 2008 and 2012 Presidential campaigns.

Senator Talent regularly writes and speaks on the subject of national defense. He is a regular contributor to National Review Online. Late last year, Senator Talent and Senator Jon Kyl co-wrote a seminal article on the condition of the military and the relationship between strategic foreign policy and national defense, titled "A Strong and Focused National Security Strategy.

Appendix 8

QDR National Defense Panel
Support Staff

Paul D. Hughes
Executive Director

Thomas A. Bowditch
Lead Writer

Project Specialist
Hanne Bursch, USIP

Shawn Brimley
Elbridge Colby
Thomas Donnelly
Mackenzie Eaglen
Thomas Mahnken
Troy Stoner

LMI Support Staff to the Panel
Charles Arnold
George Sinks

U.S. Government Liaison Officers
Lori Abele
Chief of Staff, Deputy Under Secretary of Defense for Strategy, Plans, and Forces

LTC Stephanie Ahern
Army Advisor for Strategy, Office of the DASD for Strategy, Plans, and Forces

Malia DuMont
Team Chief of Strategic Trends, Office of the DASD for Strategy, Plans, and Forces

Deana Funderburk
Legislative Affairs Specialist for DUSD for Strategy, Plans, and Forces

The Co-chairs wish to express their thanks to the following organizations through whose efforts this project
was facilitated and supported:

The United States Institute of Peace
LMI